*But there were false prophets also among the people, even as there shall be false teachers among you, who privily shall bring damnable heresies, even denying the Lord that bought them, and bring upon themselves swift destruction.*

*And many shall follow their pernicious ways; by reason of whom the way of truth shall be evil spoken of.*

*And through covetousness shall they with feigned words make merchandise of you; whose judgment now of a long time lingereth not, and their damnation slumbereth not.*

*II Peter 2:1-3*

# CHRISTIANITY CRIME AGAINST HUMANITY

By Arnold Gordon

5 Star Publishing Company
P.O. Box 0568
Galesburg, Illinois 61402


Second Printing 1992

ISBN 0-9632629-0-4

## TABLE OF CONTENTS

# CHRISTIANITY CRIME AGAINST HUMANITY

## INTRODUCTION

This work is a serious attempt to objectively compare practicing Christianity with the authentic record of the teachings of Jesus Christ and his personally designated apostles. The only available authentic record of his teachings stems from the Latin "Vulgate Bible".

The King James version Holy Bible is used for reference as it has been approved as the most authentic translation by all of organized Christendom. The Catholic Douay version Old Testament and the Confraternity version New Testament, with the Imprimatur of the Catholic Church is accepted by the author, to be accurate in translation, as well.

Although polemic in nature, this work is intended to be helpful in purpose. It is a revelation of truth, intended to rescue those found in delusion, and forewarn those would-be Christians that are truly sincere.

A review of Christianity as generally taught today, is compared in detail, with the recorded scriptures of the Holy Bible. Many deviations and customs are reviewed to determine how and why so many of these modern "Christian" practices found their way so far from the teachings of Christ.

Every attempt is made to present scriptural references, with chapter and verse location, to establish Biblical proof of the author's position on each situation covered.

This is not an attempt to establish the validity of the scriptures or Christ's teachings. The validity of Christ's teachings will stand or fall on their own merit, without the help of this author.

This work deals with whether or not Christianity of today, by its very name, is in fact representative of the Biblical record of Christ's teachings. If in fact, it is not representative of Christ's teachings, it cannot legally or otherwise represent itself as such. It is the duty and obligation of this writer, and any one else that agrees with the premise set forth here, to make every effort to expose these fraudulent acts.

It does boggle the mind to imagine how many people throughout the world are misguided and deceived by these gross misrepresentations. The depth of the affects on these misinformed sincere people is impossible to calculate.

It is high time something should be done by all of us to make some effort to protect those who are ignorant of the deceptions they find themselves in.

This work makes every effort to show plainly and reasonably the facts surrounding this hoax called Christianity. The facts speak for themselves. This is not a claim on beliefs and/or religious rights, but an open charge of factual fraud and deception of the worst sort.

Christ only taught one doctrine, and the record is clearly delineated in the Holy Bible. Even so, there are multitudes of different doctrines fraudulently claiming to be accurately based on the teachings of Christ. It is generally accepted that this is due to different interpretations of Christ's teachings. This work does not deal with interpretations, but with the misrepresentation of facts, which leaves no room for interpretation.

All groups calling themselves Christian, each being different in their teachings, cannot accurately claim they represent the one and only doctrine of Christ. With so many deviations, this work will show there are some that are obvious impostors.

The "Doctrine of the Trinity" teaches, there are three persons in the Godhead. "Webster's New World Dictionary of the American Language" provides the primary definition of person as follows: **"1. a human being, esp. as distinguished from a thing or lower animal, individual man, woman, or child".** Thus the term "person" cannot be attributed to at least two of the three entities of the so called "Trinity" or "Triune God".

The following compilation of scriptures from the Holy Bible, King James Version, will establish that the ***"Begotten Son is the only human being or person in the Godhead. God is a Spirit," (John 4:24)*** The word "Spirit" in John 4:24 was translated from the Greek word,"pneuma", meaning "vital principal, mental disposition" thus ethereal in nature, and not a person. The "Holy Ghost", or Holy Spirit, is the manifestation of the power of God in spirit form as well.

God, supernatural in being, is sovereign in purpose, and is the only supreme authority. Jesus Christ the begotten Son of God is also son of man with a special purpose. ***"For there is one God, and one mediator between God and men, the man Christ Jesus". (I Timothy 2:5)***

The following compilation of scripture will delineate the Godhead thoroughly, according to the Holy Bible. It is forever established in the word and the word cannot be broken.

# TODAY'S CHRISTIANITY

***"For the leaders of this people cause them to err: and they that are led of them are destroyed"***

***Isaiah 9:16***

Mankind is enjoying an ever increasing position of materialistic achievement in the world of today. He has harnessed the power of nuclear fission. He has challenged and overcome the heretofore insurmountable obstacles of travel in outer space. He has traveled to the moon and back safely. He has developed communications techniques which stagger the imagination of the individual. He has uncovered many secrets of the human body. Civilization has advanced beyond the most optimistic expectations of our forefathers, that is, materially speaking.

While these materialistic gains have been so astounding, the intelligence of man has dangerously receded to the point of imminent disaster. The recent years have shown man has made little or no progress in accomplishing unanimity with his brothers. Brotherhood among nations is so remote it doesn't seem to warrant serious consideration in this era. Peace in the world today remains as elusive as it ever has, in the history of man.

The individuals in today's world have increasingly less regard for one another. The common interest of the community no longer exists as it once did in our society. The manifestation of brotherly love such as a house raising or barn raising are so rare, it becomes a newsworthy story when and if such a manifestation should take place. The security of our nation and the world lie in jeopardy due to man's lack of consideration for the rights of his fellow man.

The situation has reached such proportions that the foremost concern of today's leaders, has become peace in the world, and law and order in our communities. It is widely claimed that a person is not safe to walk on the streets of our cities. For the first time in our history, authorities find themselves incapable of coping with the lawlessness of our youth throughout the world. Our nation's greatest minds remain at loss to find a solution to the explosive race problem. Even the morals, which were once cherished by the majority, have reduced nearly to the point of nonexistence.

This state of imbalance, in our world of prosperity, is due to the paradox of what is claimed to be Christianity. Although the civilized world of today is founded upon the precepts of Christianity, the practicing religion claiming that title is not Christianity, but is rather that of Materialism. A serious review of the facts will prove this to be true.

One needs only to look around himself, where he is, and consider truthfully, to realize Materialism is the motivating force in the lives of today's society.

Materialism is preoccupation with, or stress upon, material rather than intellectual or spiritual things. On the contrary, Christ gave the following commandment: ***"Lay not up for yourselves treasures upon earth, where moth and rust doth corrupt, and where thieves break through and steal: But lay up for yourselves treasures in heaven, where neither moth nor rust doth corrupt, and where thieves do not break through nor steal: For where your treasure is, there will your heart be also." (Matthew 6:19-21)*** He also sternly warned all, saying, ***"Labour not for the meat which perisheth, but for that meat which***

***endureth unto everlasting life, which the Son of man shall give unto you: for him hath God the Father sealed." (John 6:27)***

Man's failure to balance the material prosperity with intellectual and spiritual prosperity is based upon his failure to heed the sage advice of the founder of the religion he so nobly claims as his own. While claiming to be a disciple of Christ, the so-called Christian of today is pursuing a course which is anti-christian. It is no marvel that spiritual degradation exists in our society.

The true reason for this dilemma is; what is generally called Christianity today is the result of history's most despicable hoax. Man has voluntarily submitted to this fraud against humanity due to social pressures, without investigation into the fundamental foundation of his religious beliefs. Through ignorance, due to lack of teaching by today's ministers of Christ's doctrine, man finds himself going contrary to that doctrine.

A person that turns to Christianity, seeking salvation, cannot escape being overwhelmed in confusion. Christianity as practiced today is a myriad of contradictory beliefs and doctrines. Each representative group professes to be founded on the teachings of Christ. While Christianity today is represented by a multitude of doctrines, Christ was the proponent of only one simple principle. That principle was, that one could love God and man with perfect love. The prospective convert need only make a cursory inspection of the recognized representative groups of Christianity today to find it virtually impossible to pick one objectively, as the true teacher of Christ's doctrine.

A detailed study will readily reveal, Christianity today is the greatest hoax ever perpetrated against mankind since his creation. Indeed; the most prevalent indictment against modern Christianity, is the general acceptance, of the many differing "faiths" among its proclaimers. The very existence of the innumerable schisms tolerated within the sphere of Christianity proves to the intelligent objective mind that Christianity today is not representative of Christ's teachings.

Christ, himself, warned of this impending fraud while preaching the famous "Sermon on the Mount". He said, ***"Beware of false prophets, which come to you in sheep's clothing, but inwardly they are ravening wolves." (Matthew 7:15)*** The Apostle Peter also gave a similar warning when he wrote: ***"But there were false prophets also among the people, even as there shall be false teachers among you, who privily shall bring in damnable heresies, ever denying the Lord that brought them, and bring upon themselves swift destruction. And many shall follow their pernicious ways; by reason of whom the way of truth shall be evil spoken of. And through covetousness shall they with feigned words make merchandise of you: whose judgment now of a long time lingereth not, and their damnation slumbereth not." (II Peter 2:1-3)***

Apostle John also joined in warning of the inevitable when he said, ***"Beloved, believe not every spirit, but try the spirits whether they are of God; because many false prophets are gone out into the world." (I John 4:1)***

He also said, ***"Whosoever transgresseth, and abideth not in the doctrine of Christ, hath not God. He that abideth in the doctrine of Christ, he hath both the Father and the Son. If there come any unto you, and bring not this doctrine, receive him not into your house, neither bid him Godspeed: For he that biddeth him Godspeed is partaker of his evil deeds." (II John 9)*** Apostle Paul was not to remain silent in light of this imminent danger when he warned the church at Collosse, ***"Beware***

***lest any man spoil you through philosophy and vain deceit, after the tradition of men, after the rudiments of this world, and not after Christ. For in him dwelleth all the fullness of the Godhead bodily." (Colossians 2:8-9)*** Paul also became very indignant against false teachings, when he told the Galatians: ***"But though we or an angel from heaven, preach any other gospel unto you, let him be accursed." (Galatians 1:8)***

With these stern warnings from Christ himself and these personally chosen teachers of his doctrine, one need only make a comparison of the doctrine taught by Christ and his apostles to find Christianity of today a worthless imitation passed off as genuine. Indeed, in light of these warnings, all who profess Christianity would do well to evaluate the very foundations of their beliefs, as well as their teachers.

The Biblical record is the only available account of Christ's teachings. This includes the apostles' presentations of Christ's doctrine. All would-be Christians and those who call themselves Christian should study the scriptural accounts to determine whether they have succumbed to this greatest of all hoaxes. All sincere believers in a supernatural God should ask themselves the following questions:

1. What is a Christian?

2. Am I a Christian according to the teachings of Christ and his apostles?

3. Are my beliefs based on the Bible or traditions of my church?

4. What is the history and foundation of my church?

5. Is my church the one and only church as taught by Paul in his epistle to the Ephesians?

6. Does the history of all my religious customs emanate from Christ, or do some find their origin in paganism?

7. Do I believe the writers of the New Testament are the accurate portrayers of the doctrine of Christ?

A serious review of these questions should reveal to the sincere believers in God the basic foundations of his or her belief. A serious study of the New Testament will reveal whether these beliefs are based on truth or tradition.

A review of Christianity and what is called "church", today will reveal today's Christianity as syncretism. A recognizable mixture of paganism and the worship of the supernatural God of the scriptures. This is a well established fact among the learned teachers of today's Christianity, and is considered acceptable by them. Those who hold such views have become indifferent to the teachings of Christ and the apostles as well as the will of the God they profess to worship. It can well be said of them, ***"They profess to know God; but in works they deny him, being abominable, and disobedient, and unto every good work reprobate." (Titus 1:16)***

This same God gave continued warning throughout the Old Testament, to those that would be his people and would have him as their God. He warned against embracing the customs and practices of all the pagan worshippers. Christ and his apostles admonished all they came in contact with to keep his commandments. The customs and practices of the pagans were taught to be abominations to God. Yet today among the proclaimers of Christianity, many of the established abominations to God are commonly practiced as wishes of Christ. These abominations are practiced as rituals of worship to the very God that has so thoroughly denounced them.

The vast majority of those that proclaim to be Christians practice these paganistic abominations to God through ignorance of the scriptures, as well as the ignorance of paganistic worship. Many a sincere, honest-hearted individual proponent of Christianity today is blindly following a blind teacher of syncretism under the veil of Christianity.

It is no wonder that Christ exhorted the Sadducees: ***"Ye do err, not knowing the scriptures, nor the power of God." (Matthew 22:29)*** Hosea also proclaimed God's words when he declared: ***"My people are destroyed for lack of Knowledge; because thou hast rejected knowledge, I will also reject thee." (Hosea 4:6)***

This greatest of all hoaxes against mankind was designed to dupe these same, sincere, honest, God fearing individuals. Proof of this can easily be seen through a review of church history. The relevant facts, which are needed to prove the truth to the skeptic, are readily available to all. The only requirement is the desire to know the truth and the ability to read. Those that are unlearned and uneducated are the ones to be most pitied of all the victims of this fraud against mankind. It is the great paradox of our time and the past centuries that the educated and learned have fallen victim to this debauchery. As in all other hoaxes, the victim willingly is defrauded due to his own lack of suspicion or his refusal to put forth the effort to uncover the truth. He willingly submits, by blindly accepting the promises of the perpetrator without question. This is the situation with most of the proponents of today's Christianity.

A conscientious aspirant to Christianity is justifiably bewildered to find politics, jealousy, competition, greed, selfishness, hatred, and even idolatry as common practices in the churches of today's Christianity. The obvious question comes to his mind, and he asks, "How did Christ's teachings of 'love thy neighbor as thyself' develop into these gross misrepresentations of his doctrine?" The only logical conclusion he can come to is the greatest majority of churches claiming to be Christian are obvious impostors.

The writer of the book of Hebrews states with emphatic authority, ***"Jesus Christ the same yesterday, and today, and forever. Be not carried about with divers (different) and strange doctrines." (Hebrews 13:8-9)*** Since the death of Christ on the cross, man has proceeded to modify and, in his own mind, improve upon the doctrine of Christ. These efforts have been undertaken in direct defiance to what is proclaimed as the sacred writings of the New Testament. As a result, Christianity has continued to deviate from the only factual account, to a myriad of contradictions and misrepresentations.

The average person tends to rationalize this present day phenomenon called Christianity, and attribute its multiplicity of doctrines to sincere attempts to interpret the scriptures honestly. It is quite obvious, those which hold this view have not made an objective study of the New Testament, while believing the words are those of divinely inspired writers. They have failed to accept the writings of the apostles as proclaimers of Christ's message to his followers. They cannot believe the prophecy of Isaiah which declares the way shall be for those: the wayfaring men, though fools, shall not err therein.

Christ, himself, declared, ***"Except ye be converted and become as little children, ye shall not enter into the kingdom of heaven." (Matthew 18:3)*** Apostle Paul told the Corinthians, ***"For ye see your calling, brethren, how that not many wise men after the flesh, not many noble, are called: but God hath chosen the foolish things of the world to confound the wise; and God hath chosen the weak things of the world, and things which are despised, hath God chosen, yes and things which are not, to bring to nought things that are: That no flesh should glory in his presence." (I Corinthians 2: 26-29)***

If we can ascribe any validity to these words of Christ and the Apostle Paul, we can only assume the child-like individual and the unpretentious person are the only recipients of the doctrine of Christ. All other aspirants are left confounded and lost in misinterpretations. It would appear Christianity was intended from the beginning for those which would strip themselves of personal acclaim and self achievement. It is no wonder that we find the exalted and scholarly teachers of today's Christianity lost in contradictions.

The simple and unlearned find Christianity the same yesterday, today, and forever, and as real for them as it was when Christ walked the shores of Galilee. Did not Christ say unto his disciples, ***"If any man will come after me, let him deny himself." (Matthew 16:24) He also said, "He that is greatest among you shall be your servant. And whosoever shall exalt himself shall be abased; and he that shall humble himself shall be exalted." (Matthew 23:11-12)*** It is easy to see those which claim Christianity among us are being led by men who have not ceased to exalt themselves. The churches of today are pursuing a policy of self-acclaim against the very teachings of Christ.

The churches of today have entered into a competitive race in an attempt to achieve a position of prestige over their counterparts. Even the individual members are found to be actively engaged in church politics while endeavoring to attain higher office and personal recognition within the church. Paul exhorted the Philippians, ***"Let this mind be in you which was also in Christ Jesus: Who, being in the form of God, thought it not robbery to be equal with God: But made himself no reputation, and took upon him the form of a servant, and was made in the likeness of men: And being found in fashion as a man, he humbled himself, and became obedient unto death, even unto the death of the cross." (Philippians 2:5-8)*** According to his own statements, he was obedient to the will of his father, at the price of his own reputation and personal achievements.

Where is the Christian today that will take up his cross daily and follow Christ, instead of their own will, or that of another? Where is the Christian that even knows with self assurance what the teachings of Christ are? Where is the Christian that knows with positive proof he is a follower of Christ's doctrine and not traditions of men? Where is the Christian that believes all the words of the New Testament are divinely inspired and are for his teachings? Where is the Christian that has presented himself a living sacrifice, holy and acceptable unto God, which is his reasonable service? Where is the Christian that even believes he can be perfect as Christ commanded all to be?

Most ministers of today's Christianity teach that men cannot be perfect and that not all the teachings of Christ and the apostles are for us today, yet we have no record of any of his teachings or commandments ever being rescinded. No wonder he asked them, ***"Can the blind lead the blind? Shall not they both fall in the ditch?"*** *(Matthew 15:14)*

## CHURCH HISTORY

***"Fear them not therefore: for there is nothing covered, that shall not be revealed; and hid, that shall not be known."***

***Matthew 10:26***

With the vast amount of conflict and divisions of Christendom today, evidence is convincing that church leaders are often in error. To the interested observer, the gnawing question persists, "Why are there so many variations of Christianity existing in the world today?" The readily available answers seem to be infested with organizational or denominational bias, historical traditions, and personal prejudices. The searcher for truth need not look very far to find most of these answers based on unfounded legends and suppositions.

He finds himself faced with what seems to be an insurmountable obstacle. The ever gnawing question affords him the impetus needed to launch into this formidable task. The immediately obvious conclusion is: With so many divisions, denominations, conflictions, and disagreements within the framework of Christianity, all cannot be correct. In desperation, he finds himself referring to the words of the founder himself to determine which of the proclaiming representatives are in agreement with his teachings.

Preliminary research reveals the only original authoritative source of Christ's teachings is limited to the writings of the apostles which were commissioned personally by him, to propagate his doctrine. Immediately, this gives the only sound basis for the truth of Christianity. All other sources available today are subsequent to, and dependent upon the writings of the apostles recorded in the Bible.

The historians, theologians, and encyclopaedists record Christianity and the church as originating with the birth of Christ. With these overwhelming oppositions, it would appear foolhardy to challenge such an impressive array of specialists. However, instead of playing mans' favorite game of follow the leader, the seeker of truth must resort to the ultimate authority.

According to John the Revelator, Christ proclaimed, ***"I am Alpha and Omega, the beginning and the ending." (Revelations 1:8)*** Christ also admonished the Jews which challenged his authority, by claiming to be descendants of Abraham. He said, ***"Verily, verily, I say unto you, before Abraham was, I am." (John 8:58)*** He warned the Jews concerning their lack of knowledge of himself, when he said, ***"Search the scriptures; for in them ye think ye have eternal life: and they are they which testify of me." (John 5:39)***

Christ revealed his preexistence in his prayer to the Father when he said, ***"I have glorified thee on the earth: I have finished the work which thou gavest me to do. And now, O' Father glorify thou me with thine own self with the glory which I had with thee before the world was." (John 17:4-5)*** John described this preexistence in this way, ***"In the beginning was the Word, and the Word was with God, and the Word was God. The same was in the beginning with God." (John 1:1-2) "And the Word was made flesh, and dwelt among us, (and we beheld his glory, the glory as of the only begotten of the Father), full of grace and truth." (John 1:14)***

Thus, his own words and those of his apostle establish the

existence of Christ in some form or state prior to his appearance in the fleshly form of the begotten son. It is reasonable to ask then, does not Christianity actually begin with the beginning of Christ rather than with his birth in the flesh of man?

Christ, himself, gives us the answer with these words, ***"When the Son of man shall come in his glory, and all the holy angels with him, then shall he sit upon the throne of his glory: And before him shall be gathered all nations: and he shall separate them one from another, as a shepherd divideth his sheep from the goats: And he shall set the sheep on his right hand, but the goats on the left. Then shall the King say unto them on his right hand, Come, ye blessed of my Father, inherit the kingdom prepared for you from the foundation of the world." (Matthew 25:31-34)***

The writer to the Hebrews reiterates, ***"For we which have believed do enter into rest, as he said, As I have sworn in my wrath, if they shall enter into my rest: although the works were finished from the foundation of the world." (Hebrew 4:3)***

Apostle Paul sheds more light with these words to the Ephesians, ***"Blessed be the God and Father of our Lord Jesus Christ, who hath blessed us with all spiritual blessings in heavenly places in Christ: According as he hath chosen us in him before the foundation of the world, that we should be holy and without blame before him in love: Having predestinated us unto the adoption of children by Jesus Christ to himself, according to the good pleasure of his will." (Ephesians 1:3-5)***

The question arises. If Christ's Kingdom was prepared from the foundation of the world, is there any basis for the belief that the followers of Christ are limited to only those born since the comparatively recent birth of the begotten son. The writer to the

Hebrews gives us a view into the eschatological hope of those described as righteous, who lived before the birth of the begotten son.

He states, ***"These all died in faith, not having received the promises, but having seen them afar off, and were persuaded of them, and embraced them, and confessed that they were strangers and pilgrims on the earth. For they that say such things declare plainly that they seek a country. And truly, if they had been mindful of that country from whence they came out, they might have had opportunity to have returned. But now they desire a better country, that is, an heavenly: Wherefore God is not ashamed to be called their God: For he hath prepared for them a city." (Hebrews 11:13-16)***

Further study reveals this city prepared for God's chosen people which lived before Christ's appearance as man on earth, is the same Kingdom prepared from the foundation of the World. Although Christ was not born into the world as the only begotten son until approximately 2000 years ago, he was active in the lives of the believers long before then.

Again, Paul confirms this in his letter to the Corinthians in which he wrote, ***"Moreover, brethren, I would not that ye should be ignorant, how that all our fathers were under the cloud, and all passed through the sea; And were all baptized unto Moses in the cloud and in the sea; And did all eat the same spiritual meat; And did all drink the same spiritual drink: for they drank of the spiritual Rock that followed them: and that Rock was Christ.***

***But with many of them God was not well pleased: for they were overthrown in the wilderness. Now these things were our examples, to the intent we should not lust after evil things,***

*as they also lusted. Neither be ye idolaters, as were some of them; as it is written, 'the people sat down to eat and drink, and rose up to play.' Neither let us commit fornication, as some of them committed, and fell in one day three and twenty thousand. Neither let us tempt Christ, as some of them also tempted, and were destroyed of serpents. Neither murmur ye, as some of them also murmured, and were destroyed of the destroyer.*

*Now all these things happened unto them for examples: and they are written for our admonition, upon whom the ends of the world are come." (I Corinthians 10:1-11)* Paul also wrote to the Romans these words, *"For whatsoever things were written aforetime were written for our learning, that we through patience and comfort of the scriptures might have hope." (Romans 15:4)*

Paul encouraged Timothy when he said, *"And that from a child thou hast known the holy scriptures* (Old Testament), *which are able to make thee wise unto salvation through faith which is in Christ Jesus. All scripture is given by inspiration of God, and is profitable for doctrine, for reproof, for correction, for instruction in righteousness: That the man of God may be perfect, thoroughly furnished unto all good works." (II Timothy 3:15-17)*

Although those that lived prior to the birth of Christ were definitely in a different set of circumstances, church history cannot leave them out of Christianity. Indeed, without the lives and examples set by them, there could be no Christianity subsequent to Christ's birth.

Talking to those of both eras, namely Gentiles under Christ, and Jews under the law, Paul wrote in his letter to the Ephesians:

*"But now in Christ Jesus ye who sometimes were far off are made nigh by the blood of Christ. For he is our peace, who hath made both one, and hath broken down the middle wall of partition between us; having abolished in his flesh the enmity, even the law of commandments contained in ordinances: for to make in himself of twain one new man, so making peace.*

*And that he might reconcile both unto God in one body by the cross, having slain the enmity thereby: And came and preached peace to you which were afar off, and to them that were nigh. For through him we both have access by one Spirit unto the Father.*

*Now therefore ye are no more strangers and foreigners, but fellow citizens with the saints, and of the household of God; And are built upon the foundation of the apostles and prophets, Jesus Christ himself being the chief corner stone; In whom all the building fitly framed together groweth unto an holy temple in the Lord: in whom ye also are builded together for an habitation of God through the Spirit." (Ephesians 2:13-22)*

According to these words and the rest of the scriptures, Christ did not come to establish a new religion or "church". But rather he came to establish the foundation which was already laid by his forefathers in the flesh. His death on the cross merely completed the "church" which had its beginning from the foundation of the world. He could now say, "it is finished."

We find then, he bridged the gap between the church of the Old Testament era and the church of the New Testament era. He thus maintained the continuity of church history from the foundation of the world. It is also found, the scriptures and events marking the period of Christ's preexistence are deemed necessary and beneficial to the fulfillment of the Christian life. Therefore, church history as well as Christianity are inseparable from what is generally referred to as Judaism.

Although the writers of history have chosen to distinguish a separation between Judaism and Christianity, a careful study of Christ's own words will uncover their error. He said, ***"Think not that I am come to destroy the law, or the prophets: I am not come to destroy, but to fulfil. For verily I say unto you, Till heaven and earth pass, one jot or one tittle shall in no wise pass from the law, till all be fulfilled." (Matthew 5:17-18)*** It should be pointed out, that in spite of the error of historians, theologians, and encyclopaedists, many proclaimers of Christianity recognize a necessary significance in the Old Testament writings. Peter wrote these words to all Christians, ***"This second epistle, beloved, I now write unto you; in both which I stir up your pure minds by way of remembrance: That ye may be mindful of the words which were spoken before by the holy prophets, and to the commandment of us the apostles of the Lord and Saviour." (II Peter 3:1-2)***

Not unlike the church of today, the church during the period of Christ's ministry was in the throws of apostasy. He found it necessary to warn them with these words: ***"But woe unto you, Pharisees! for ye tithe mint and rue and all manner of herbs, and pass over judgment and the love of God: these ought ye to have done, and not to leave the other undone. Woe unto you. Pharisees! for ye love the uppermost seats in the synagogues, and greetings in the markets. Woe unto you, scribes and Pharisees, hypocrites! for ye are as graves which appear not, and the men that walk over them are not aware of them.***

***Woe unto you also, ye lawyers! for ye lade men with***

*burdens grievous to be borne, and ye yourselves touch not the burdens with one of your fingers. Woe unto you! for ye build the sepulchres of the prophets, and your fathers killed them. Truly ye bear witness that ye allow the deeds of your fathers: for they indeed killed them, and ye build their sepulchres.*

*Therefore also said the wisdom of God, 'I will send them prophets and apostles and some of them they shall slay and persecute': that the blood of all the prophets, which was shed from the foundation of the world, may be required of this generation; From the blood of Abel unto the blood of Zacharias, which perished between the altar and the temple: verily I say unto you, It shall be required of this generation. Woe unto you lawyers! for ye have taken away the key of knowledge: ye entered not in yourselves, and them that were entering in ye hindered." (Luke 11:42-52)* Then as well as now, the church was infested with self-righteousness, deceit, personal acclaim, hypocrisy and vanity. Then as well as now pretenders made a concerted effort to cover their spiritual deficiency with an outward cloak of piety. As in the days of Christ's ministry, doctrines as well as personal beliefs are based on misinterpretation of scripture, personal feelings, and desires of the flesh.

Solomon in his wisdom assured all, *"There is a way which seemeth right unto a man, but the end thereof are the ways of death." (Proverbs 14:12)* He also stated, *"The way of a fool is right in his own eyes." (Proverbs 12:15)* Isaiah declared, *"For my thoughts are not your thoughts, neither are your ways my ways, saith the Lord. For as the heavens are higher than the earth, so are my ways higher than your ways, and my thoughts than your thoughts." (Isaiah 55:8-9)* Solomon exhorted saying, *"Trust in the Lord with all thine heart; and lean not unto thine*

***own understanding." (Proverbs 3:5)*** Therefore, doctrines and beliefs based on man's ways cannot result in the Salvation of the soul. Christ gave the answer to all who would hear, when he said: ***"It is the spirit that quickeneth; the flesh profiteth nothing: the words that I speak unto you, they are spirit, and they are life." (John 6:63)***

Down through the ages all history reveals that any group, (ethnic or religious) which did not conform to the popular ways of his contemporaries was rejected. This was the case with the Children of Israel in Egypt before the exodus. This was the primary reason Christ was rejected, regardless of his exemplary life and the miracles he performed. The apostles and the New Testament Christians experienced this in the persecutions of the church. The true follower of God's Word has always been rejected for his refusal to conform to man's ways.

Christ spoke of the true Christian when he said, ***"They are not of the world, even as I am not of the world. Sanctify them through thy truth: thy word is truth." (John 17:16-17)*** He assured them, ***"If the world hate you, ye know that it hated me before it hated you. If ye were of the world, the world would love his own: but because ye are not of the world, but I have chosen you out of the world, therefore the world hateth you." (John 15:18-19)***

Since the beginning, the apostate church has sought the favor and recognition of the world. The "True Church" recognized the inherent conflict of principles between the believer and the world which pursues the ways of man. The believer has always rejected man's ways, including those of himself, and seeks to follow the ways of God, as depicted in His Word. The apostate church in these last days are preaching the world in the church and the church is the world. They have come to measure salvation in the terms and the ways of the world. They preach against the disassociation of the Christian from the world and its customs and traditions.

The apostate church has ceased to rely exclusively on God's Word. Instead, they have injected man's thoughts and philosophy into the interpretation of God's Word. The result has become as faceted as the many different minds injected into modern Theology. Unity of purpose cannot be achieved as long as man's ways and man's philosophy is included in the leadership and doctrinal teachings of Christianity. Theology breeds conflict and confusion between those of different philosophical concepts of God's Word. This is due to the unwillingness to accept the Word of God at face value.

Apostle James gave stern warning to these religious deviates. He said, ***"From whence come wars and fightings among you? Come they not hence, even of your lusts that war in your members? Ye lust, and have not: ye kill, and desire to have, and cannot obtain: ye fight and war, yet ye have not, because ye ask not. Ye ask, and receive not, because ye ask amiss, that ye may consume it upon your lusts.***

***Ye adulterers and adulteresses, know ye not that the friendship of the world is enmity with God? Whosoever therefore will be a friend of the world is the enemy of God. Do ye think that the scripture saith in vain. The spirit that dwelleth in us lusteth to envy?" (James 4:1-5)***

Jeremiah prophetically made this comparison between the believer and the world. ***"Thus saith the Lord; Cursed be the man that trusteth in man, and maketh flesh his arm, and whose heart departeth from the Lord. For he shall be like the heath in the desert, and shall not see when good cometh; but shall inhabit***

***the parched places in the wilderness, in a salt land and not inhabited.***

***Blessed is the man that trusteth in the Lord, and whose hope the Lord is. For he shall be as a tree planted by the waters, and that spreadeth out her roots by the river, and shall not see when heat cometh, but her leaf shall be green; and shall not be careful in the year of drought, neither shall cease from yielding fruit. The heart is deceitful and desperately wicked: who can know it." (Jeremiah 17:5-9)***

In the study of the only universally recognized authoritative source of Christ's teachings; (the Bible) the searcher of truth finds the seed of the apostate church of today already flourishing and rooted. Christ, himself, warned, ***"Beware of false prophets, which come to you in sheep's clothing, but inwardly they are ravening wolves." (Matthew 7:15)*** The Apostle Peter also gave a similar warning when he wrote: ***"But there were false prophets also among the people, even as there shall be false teachers among you, who privily shall bring in damnable heresies, even denying the Lord that brought them, and bring upon themselves swift destruction. And many shall follow their pernicious ways; by reason of whom the way of truth shall be evil spoken of. And through covetousness shall they with feigned words make merchandise of you: whose judgment now of a long time lingereth not, and their damnation slumbereth not." (II Peter 2:1-3)***

Paul detected this seed of apostasy sprouting in the Church of Corinth. This is witnessed by these words of warning to the Corinthians: ***"Now I beseech you, brethren, by the name of our Lord Jesus Christ, that ye shall speak the same thing, and that there be no divisions among you; but that ye be perfectly***

***joined together in the same mind and in the same judgment. For it hath been declared unto me of you, my brethren, by them which are of the house of Chloe, that there are contentions among you." (I Corinthians 1:10-11)*** Again he said to them: ***"For ye are yet carnal: for whereas there is among you envying, and strife, and divisions, are ye not carnal, and walk as men?" (I Corinthians 3:3)*** Paul saw that the divisions which already existed could not be allowed to continue. He knew such divisions breed only greater deviations and ultimately heretical apostasy. Unfortunately, history has convinced us apostasy came despite their warnings. Christendom today is suffering from the very same characteristics that Paul so judiciously warned against.

After a close study of the teachings of Christ it is easy to see the growth of apostasy flourished in parallel with the exalting of the individual. Christ set the example for his followers, taking on the form of a servant. He showed his humility when he, the "Lord and Master" washed the Apostles' feet. Peter followed this example of humility and would not allow Cornelius to fall down at his feet and worship him, saying, ***"stand up; I myself also am a man." (Acts 10:26)***

Contrast these examples of humility and the refusal of the apostles to establish themselves as lords over God's heritage with those claiming to be "The Church" since the days of the Apostles. Many claim to be the true successors of Christ and the Apostles. One need only examine the authoritative evidence, to find the true Church. Should not the proclaimers of Christianity follow in the footsteps of Christ and the Apostles?

Since the fourth century the so-called church has been marked with arrogant lordship over its members according to the commandments and traditions of men contrary to the teachings of

Christ and his apostles. The apostate church has continually sought publicity and affinity with the world. Christ warned His followers with these Words: ***"And ye shall be hated of all men for my names sake: but he that endureth to the end shall be saved." (Matthew 10:22)*** He continued, ***"the disciple is not above His master, nor the servant above his lord. It is enough for the disciple that he be as His master, and the servant as his lord. If they called the master of the house Beelzebub, how much more shall they call them of his household? Fear them not therefore: for there is nothing covered, that shall not be revealed; and hid, that shall not be known." (Matthew 10:24-26)***

A close study into the personality and divine nature of a disciple of Christ and the Apostles, according to the scriptures, will contrast that nature and personality of the impostor. It cannot be conceived from the scriptures that any disciple of Christ would embark upon a policy of annihilation of his fellow man regardless of his crime.

Christ said, ***"But I say unto you, love your enemies, bless them that curse you, do good to them that hate you, and pray for them which despitefully use you, and persecute you; that ye may be the children of your Father which is in heaven: For he maketh his sun to rise on the evil and on the good, and sendeth rain on the just and the unjust. For if ye love them which love you, what reward have ye? do not even the publicans the same? And if ye salute your brethren only, what do ye more than others? do not even the publicans so?" (Matthew 5:44-47)*** Has this been the doctrine and the practice of the historical church?

Paul told the Romans, ***"Bless them which persecute you: bless, and curse not. Rejoice with them that do rejoice, and***

***weep with them that weep. Be of the same mind one toward another. Mind not high things, but condescend to men of low estate. Be not wise in your own conceits. Recompense to no man evil for evil. Provide things honest in the sight of all men.***

***If it be possible, as much as lieth in you, live peaceably with all men. Dearly beloved, avenge not yourselves, but rather give place unto wrath: for it is written, 'Vengeance is mine' saith the Lord. Therefore if thine enemy hunger, feed him; if he thirst, give him drink: for in so doing thou shalt heap coals of fire on his head. Be not overcome of evil, but overcome evil with good." (Romans 12:14-21)***

Are these the attributes of the historical church which claims to be the adherent of Christ's example and doctrine? The true disciple of Christ has continually served God obscurely. Because of his obscure way of life, he is not generally accepted. His inherent divine nature finds him alone and separated from those who ascribe to the ways of the world.

Moses instructed the "Children of Israel" in the wilderness, adding, ***"For thou art an holy people unto the Lord thy God, and the Lord hath chosen thee to be a peculiar people unto himself, above all the nations that are upon the earth." (Deuteronomy 14:2)*** Apostle Peter echoed these words to the New Testament church, saying, ***"But ye are a chosen generation, a royal priesthood, an holy nation, a peculiar people; that ye should show forth the praises of him who hath called you out of darkness into his marvelous light." (I Peter 2:9)*** Can a person follow Christ and the world at the same time? Have the historians accurately depicted "The Church"?

One is forced to question, whether the Crusades, the

Inquisition, martyring, or other such atrocious behavior would be condoned by the bearer of peace and love to all mankind, including his enemies. Should not the disciple of Christ be content to wage spiritual war against his enemies? Apostle Paul explained the Christian's battle in this manner: ***"Finally my brethren, be strong in the Lord, and in the power of his might. Put on the whole armour of God, that ye may be able to stand against the wiles of the devil. For we wrestle not against flesh and blood, but against principalities, against powers, against the rulers of the darkness of this world, against spiritual wickedness in high places.***

***Wherefore take unto you the whole armour of God, that ye may be able to withstand in the evil day, and having done all, to stand. Stand therefore, having your loins girt about with truth, and having on the breastplate of righteousness; and your feet shod with the preparation of the gospel of peace; Above all, taking the shield of faith, wherewith ye shall be able to quench all the fiery darts of the wicked. And take the helmet of salvation, and the sword of the Spirit, which is the Word of God. Praying always with all prayer and supplication for all saints." (Ephesians 6:10-18)*** This certainly doesn't sound like the battle array of the Crusaders and the Inquisitioners. Did they not wear the battle array of the armies of the world? Could they have been the bearers of the gospel of peace?

# PAGANISM IN THE CHURCHES

***"Wherefore, as I live, saith the Lord God; Surely, because thou hath defiled my sanctuary with all thy detestable things, and with all thine abominations, therefore will I also diminish thee; neither shall mine eye spare, neither will I have any pity."***

*Ezekiel 5:11*

Many modern Christians are not at all aware of the paganistic practices they partake of regularly in their Christian worship services, and in their every day way of life. Through this ignorance, many lay members are being led in worship services that are, in fact, abominable to their God. It is little wonder many find it hard to believe God hears and answers prayers.

When confronted with the paganistic aspects of today's Christianity, many of its leaders will loudly proclaim, these abominable customs are acceptable today as long as we practice them while worshipping our God. These blind leaders of the blind are in direct contradiction with Gods own words which he stated to the children of Israel for our example.

He said, ***"Ye shall therefore keep my statutes and my judgments, and shall not commit any of these abominations neither any of your own nation, nor any stranger that sojourneth among you: (For all these abominations have the men of the land done, which were before you, and the land is defiled;) That the land spew not you out also, when ye defile it, as it spewed out the nations that were before you. For***

***whosoever shall commit any of these abominations, even the souls that commit them shall be cut off from among their people. Therefore shall ye keep mine ordinance, that ye commit not any one of these abominable customs, which were committed before you, and that ye defile not yourselves therein: I am the Lord your God." (Leviticus 18:26-30)***

In prophesying God's words, Ezekiel also declared, ***"But as for them whose heart walketh after the heart of their detestable things and their abominations, I will recompense their way upon their own heads, saith the Lord God." (Ezekiel 11:21)*** He also declared, ***"Then shall they know that I am the Lord, when I have laid the land most desolate because of all their abominations which they have committed." (Ezekiel 33:29)***

In his word, God made it very plain, one of the most detestable abominations was that of "Idolatry". In today's Christian society the acceptable definition of Idolatry is limited to, "the act of kneeling or bowing and doing worship to a physical form or image". Even though God's word does not limit Idolatry to this definition, some prominent Christian churches practice this paganistic custom in utter disregard to God's word.

Apostle Paul proclaimed that "Covetousness" is Idolatry. Webster defines Covetousness as "having a craving for possession". Many sincere Christians of today ignorantly train their children to be covetous and practice Idolatry from the time of their birth. Even before a child is born, many well meaning parents procure a harmless, cuddly, image of a dog, a teddy bear or some other animal, and proceed to teach the infant to covet this "cute little toy". Some well meaning parents are so successful, the child will love, cherish, and idolize this image so much, it will not go to bed without it, and cannot feel secure unless it is in his or her possession. With such assiduous training in "Material Idolatry", it is no marvel that Christianity has taken on the contrary form of materialism.

This training in Covetousness is continued throughout the child's life with presents for birthday, Christmas, Easter, Mother's Day, Father's Day, and any other occasion the merchants can dream up. A child is taught to pursue material prosperity, and lay aside treasures upon this earth. Success in life is measured not by one's faith in God or his spiritual achievement, but rather in his material prosperity. Starting with his entrance into this world, well meaning Christian parents raise them contrary to the teachings of Christ. All with the blessings and approval of the blind teachers of today's Christianity.

Idolatrous practices do not end with materialism. The very symbolic image of Christianity finds its origin in ancient paganism. God gave stern warning to the Children of Israel, forbidding idolatry when he said, ***"I am the Lord thy God which have brought thee out of the land of Egypt, out of the house of bondage. Thou shalt have no other gods before me. Thou shalt not make unto thee any graven image, or any likeness of anything that is in heaven above, or that is in the earth beneath, or that is in the water under the earth: Thou shalt not bow down thyself to them, nor serve them: for I the Lord thy God am a jealous God." (Exodus 20:2-5)***

We find today that Christianity has, as its symbol a paganistic image of worship, the cross. This practice is carried on in direct defiance to the above Words of God. It was not always the symbol of Christianity. We would be led to believe the cross was used as a symbol of Christianity only since Christ was crucified at

Calvary. A review of history will show the image of the cross was introduced as a symbol of Christianity by Emperor Constantine in the fourth century. Crosses were not used in churches of Christendom until the fifth century.

The origin of the cross as a pagan symbol of worship and the practice of kissing and bowing to it dates back to ancient Babylonian times, hundreds of years before Christ. History tells us the first cross appeared as a symbol of the Babylonian Sun God Tammuz. Babylon is known to be the birth place of all pagan religions. It is no wonder, that with the paganistic practices of Christianity today, some modern theologians are teaching Babylon was also the source of Christianity.

It is true, the apostles referred to the cross of Christ. However, in light of the harsh warning of God to the Children of Israel, one can see the agony and redemption of the cross was preached; not the symbolic image.

By the same reference, the act of bowing and kissing any image is in defiance to Gods will. Christ never taught his followers to defy or disobey the Word of God. Moses forewarned all against these pagan practices of worship when he said, ***"And the Lord commanded me at that time to teach you statutes and judgments, that ye might do them in the land whither ye go over to possess it. Take ye therefore good heed unto yourselves; for ye saw no manner of similitude on the day that the Lord spake unto you in Horeb out of the midst of the fire: lest ye corrupt yourselves, and make you a graven image, the similitude of any figure, the likeness of male or female, the likeness of any beast that is on the earth, the likeness of any winged fowl that flieth in the air, the likeness of anything that creepeth on the ground, the likeness of any fish that is in the*** *waters beneath the earth: and lest thou lift up thine eyes unto heaven, and when thou seest the sun, and the moon, and the stars, even all the host of heaven, shouldest be driven to worship them, and serve them, which the Lord thy God hath divided unto all the nations under the whole heaven." (Deuteronomy 4:14-19)*

Christ taught all his followers to obey the commandments of God. The apostles taught we should obey the Word of God and not displease God as the children of Israel did by their disobedience. Therefore, it is clearly established that all images, relics, pictures, symbols, and edifices were not meant to have any place in Christianity. Instead, these are abominable items of worship which belong to paganism.

God also said, *"Remember the sabbath day, to keep it holy. Six days shalt thou labour, and do all thy work: But the seventh day is the sabbath of the Lord thy God: in it thou shalt not do any work, thou, nor thy son, nor thy daughter, thy manservant, nor thy maidservant, nor thy cattle, nor any stranger that is within thy gates: For six days the Lord made heaven and earth, the sea, and all that in them is, and rested the seventh day: wherefore the Lord blessed the sabbath day, and hallowed it." (Exodus 20:8-11)*

Thus, as one of the "Ten Commandments", God commanded that the seventh day of the week was the sabbath day and should be held in higher esteem than any other day of the week. He made it a holy day, to be set aside in memory of his rest after creation.

Isaiah records God's words this way, *"If thou turn away thy foot from the sabbath, from doing thy pleasure on my holy day; and call the sabbath a delight, the holy of the Lord,*

***honourable; and shalt honour him, not doing thine own ways, nor finding thine own pleasure, nor speaking thine own words: Then shalt thou delight thyself in the Lord; and I will cause thee to ride upon the high places of the earth, and feed thee with the heritage of Jacob thy father: for the mouth of the Lord hath spoken it." (Isaiah 58:13-14)***

God never changed his position on this throughout the entire record of the scriptures. There is no record in the scriptures where he made Sunday to take precedence over the seventh day.

The Catholic Church, however, found it convenient to make the first day of the week the holy day, and esteem it more highly than any other day of the week. This, they did in direct opposition to the wishes of God himself, and his eternal word, which cannot be broken. His commandments still are in force whether the churches follow them or not.

The Catholic Church being founded after the precepts of Paganism gave more credence to the customs of the Pagan worshippers than to the commandments of God to true Christians. Sunday, the first day of the week had always been held in higher esteem than the other days of the week by the Pagans. The first day of the week was the Sun God's day, thus the name Sunday.

The way the Catholics accomplished this is crude but successful. The only reference or reasoning that the Catholic Church uses to justify changing the holy day of the week to the first day of the week instead of the seventh day is the declaration that Christ resurrected on the first day of the week. A simple examination of the scriptures used to come to this conclusion will reveal that it is a despicable deception. The evidence is still there in the scriptures.

The scriptures used for their reference reads as follows:

***"The first day of the week cometh Mary Magdalene early, when it was yet dark, unto the sepulchre, and seeth the stone taken away from the sepulchre." (John 20:1)*** This scripture does not say Christ raised from the dead on the first day of the week, only that was when they discovered him gone.

If Christ's own words are to be accepted as truth, then he had to have risen on the evening before on the seventh day of the week. Jesus Christ predicted the time of his own resurrection when he said, ***"An evil and adulterous generation seeketh after a sign; and there shall no sign be given to it, but the sign of the prophet Jonas: For as Jonas was three days and three nights in the whale's belly; so shall the son of man be three days and three nights in the heart of the earth." (Matthew 12:39-40)***

Thus, according to Christ's own words he would resurrect at the same time of day that he was buried. He was buried on the evening of his crucifixion which had to be the evening of the fourth day of the week. Therefore, he resurrected on the seventh day of the week, not the first day.

All churches that follow the worship of Sunday as the sabbath day have been deceived, and are following the teachings of false Christianity against God's will.

Easter Sunday is considered by those in Christendom as a most important day of worship, second only to Christmas, the falsely proclaimed birthday of Christ. Many so-called Christians remember their avowed religion on these two occasions, if not during the rest of the year.

The average professing Christian takes part in the traditional customs of Easter Sunday without the slightest knowledge of how these customs originated. How many so-called Christians know the purpose of Easter sunrise service, Easter rabbits, Easter eggs, new clothes, ham dinners?

How many "Christians" know that Easter was celebrated thousands of years before the birth of Christ? Where did the holiday get the name of Easter? These questions can be answered for anyone that would take the time to go to a library and do a little research.

The word Easter is the English spelling of the word Ishtar. This was the name of the pagan "Queen of Heaven", the Mother of Life, or the Goddess of Fertility.

The customs of Easter eggs and the Easter rabbit are associated with this holiday due to their life giving re-productive characteristics. The inference that the Easter Rabbit laid the Easter Eggs is a very "unchristian falsehood" picked up along the way.

The annual Easter Parade and donning the new clothes is another unchristian custom attributed to the celebration of the return of "Nimrod", the sun god, at this time of the year.

The custom of eating ham dinner on Easter Sunday results from the feud which developed between the Roman church and the early Christian church made up primarily of Jews. The practice developed at the time of the Nicene Council (325 A.D.) to show contempt for Jewish customs.

Easter Sunrise Service is an ancient pagan custom which was incorporated into the traditions of Easter in an attempt to represent the resurrection of Christ. The truth is, this was a pagan service commemorating the return of "Nimrod" the Sun God. This practice was condemned by the Word of God.

Ezekiel wrote, ***"And he brought me into the inner court of the Lord's house, and, behold, at the door of the temple of the Lord, between the porch and the altar, were about five and twenty men, with their backs toward the temple of the Lord,***

***and their faces toward the east; and they worshipped the sun toward the east.***

***Then he said unto me, Hast thou seen this, O son of man? Is it a light thing to the house of Judah that they commit the abominations which they commit here? for they have filled the land with violence, and have returned to provoke me to anger: and, lo, they put the branch to their nose. Therefore will I also deal in fury: mine eye shall not spare, neither will I have pity: and though they cry in mine ears with a loud voice, yet will I not hear them." (Ezekiel 8:16-18)***

To compound this anti-Christian falsehood of Easter, we are told to believe that Christ was crucified on Friday and rose on "Easter" Sunday morning. Every would-be Christian need only look in his Bible to see this is the greatest falsehood of all. Christ was crucified the day before the seventh day of the "Feast of unleavened Bread" which was the "Preparation", the sixth day of the Feast of Unleavened Bread. The first day of the feast of unleavened bread was decreed by God as a sabbath day or a day of holy convocation. He, also, declared the seventh day of the feast of unleavened bread as a sabbath day, or high day. This was the same sabbath day which came the day after Jesus was crucified.

***"These are the feasts of the Lord, even holy convocations, which ye shall proclaim in their seasons. In the fourteenth day of the first month (Jewish calendar) at even is the Lord's Passover. And on the fifteenth day of the same month is the feast of unleavened bread unto the Lord: seven days ye shall eat unleavened bread.***

***In the first day ye shall have an holy convocation: ye shall do no servile work therein. But ye shall offer an offering made by fire unto the Lord seven days: in the seventh day is an***

***holy convocation: ye shall do no servile work therein". (Leviticus 23:4-8)***

John recorded the day of Jesus' crucifixion, saying, ***"The Jews therefore, because it was the preparation, that the bodies should not remain upon the cross on the sabbath day, (for that sabbath day was an high day,) besought Pilate that their legs might be broken, and that they might be taken away." (John 19:31)***

This is confirmed by the words of Christ himself when He said, ***"For as Jonas was three days and three nights in the whale's belly; so shall the Son of man be three days and three nights in the heart of the earth." (Matthew 12:40)*** It is not possible for Christ to have been buried on Friday evening and be resurrected Sunday morning, less than two days and two nights, in the earth. The angel, at the tomb, assured all that Christ kept His word. He said, ***"He is not here: for he is risen, as he said." (Matthew 28:6)***

The scriptures prove conclusively that Christ was crucified on Wednesday and was resurrected on Saturday. He did not rise from the dead along with the rising sun as Christendom has been deceived into believing. Apostle John sets the record straight with these words, ***"The first day of the week cometh Mary Magdalene early, when it was yet dark unto the sepulchre, and seeth the stone taken away from the sepulchre." (John 20:1)***

How can a true Christian worship "in spirit and in truth" amid such an array of lies and abominable practices?

Jesus said in St. John 8:31-32, ***"If ye continue in my word, then are ye my disciples indeed: And ye shall know the truth and the truth shall make you free."***

1. What is the truth about Chritmas?

2. When was Christ's birthday first celebrated?

3. Is there any scripture in the Old Testament or the New Testament to support the celebration of a mass for Christ's birth?

4. Did Christ ever teach us to remember his birthday?

5. What spiritual value is gained in the celebration of Christ's birthday?

6. Should tradition be continued even though it is not based on the truth?

7. Why is the truth not taught to the followers of today's "Ministers of Truth"?

The answers to these questions and many others should be established in the minds of today's "Ministers of Truth," lest they be guilty of blindly leading the blind into the ditch. A thorough search of the facts is in order. Year after year the effects of the holiday season have an ever increasing influence on our way of life. Year after year less emphasis is placed on the birth of Christ and more on the merry-making and material aspects of the holiday season.

The word Christmas means "Mass for Christ". The word "Mass" defined in Webster's New Twentieth Century unabridged dictionary is as follows:

"The celebration or service of the Eucharist, a sacrament of the Roman Catholic Church consisting of a series of prayers and ceremonies."

History records the earliest celebration for Christ's birthday was not until some four hundred years after his death on the cross. In the fifth Century, the Roman Catholic Church commanded the birth of Christ was to be observed forever on December 25th; the same day of the old Roman feast of the birth of Sol which was the Sun God of the ancient Romans. Christ's birthdate was thus arbitrarily established at the time of the Winter Solstice which was the same time the Roman pagan feast of Saturnalia was already being celebrated for many centuries prior to the birth of Christ. One needs only to study the ancient customs of this pagan holiday feast to find the origin of today's Christmas celebration customs which are so ignorantly associated with the birth of our Lord Jesus.

The well known Christmas customs, such as, the Christmas Tree, the Yule Log, the Mistletoe, and the Holly Berries, all have their origins stemming from pagan rituals in the worship of the Sun God. These rituals date back many centuries prior to the birth of Christ. None of these customs are in any way associated with the birth of Christ in the Biblical record of our Lord's birth. The custom of the gross falsehood of Santa Claus does not warrant consideration in a religious discussion.

The custom of the Christmas tree and yule log dates back to the origin of the pagan Sun God of Babylonian times. Nimrod a great grandson of Noah and self proclaimed Sun God, is purported to have been reincarnated into a log, out of which sprang an evergreen tree overnight, thus establishing the foundation for the Sun God Tammuz. Since that time, an evergreen tree was used as the idolatrous symbol of Tammuz. It became the custom for pagan worshippers to cut an evergreen tree and decorate it with symbols of life and reproduction such as eggs. This idolatrous ritual was always performed at the time of the Winter Solstice the very time the Roman Catholic Church decreed the celebration of our Lord's birth. By this decree, the door was opened for the decadent church to welcome idol worshippers into its fold along with the idolatrous rituals and ceremonies now prevalent in the Roman Catholic Church. This was done in direct contradiction to the "Word of God".

Jeremiah warned the house of Israel, hundreds of years before Christ's birth, concerning the idolatrous practice or custom of what is now called a Christmas tree.

***"Thus saith the Lord, learn not the way of the heathen, and be not dismayed at the signs of heaven; for the heathen are dismayed at them. For the customs of the people are vain: for one cutteth a tree out of the forest, the hands of the workman with the axe. They deck it with silver and with gold; they fasten it with nails and with hammers, that it move not. They are upright as the palm tree, but speak not; they must needs be borne, because they cannot go. Be not afraid of them; for they cannot do evil, neither also is it in them to do good." (Jeremiah 10:2-5)***

Because the people failed to heed the prophetic warnings of Jeremiah in this and other heathenistic customs, Jerusalem and all Judea were destroyed in the "Abomination of Desolation" which was a type of the end time for the New Testament Church.

God Commended the Children of Israel, ***"And in all things that I have said unto you be circumspect: and make no mention of the name of other gods, neither let it be heard out of thy mouth." (Exodus 23:13)***

Certainly, with this commandment in mind, the "True Minister of Truth" could not condone pagan celebrations in the name of our Lord and Saviour Jesus Christ. If, after knowing the truth one could still be a partaker of this Roman Catholic pagan celebration it can only be assumed they fit the category which Paul described to Timothy, ***"Now the Spirit speaketh expressly, that in the latter times some shall depart from the faith, giving heed to seducing spirits, and doctrines of devils; Speaking lies in hypocrisy; having their conscience seared with a hot iron." (I Timothy 4:1-2)***

The truth of the matter is: The true birthdate of Christ has never been accurately established. The date cannot be determined by scripture, neither in the Old Testament or the New Testament. If Christ had intended that we celebrate his birthdate, would he not have left definite instructions, as he did concerning his death?

Theologians and historians have never agreed on the exact date of Christ's birth. On the contrary, the one thing the majority agreed upon, is the fact that Christ's birthdate is not December 25th. Does not the conscience of the "Minister of Truth" tell him that it is wrong to teach his followers to partake of a lie? How can the conscience of the "Minister of Truth" allow him to teach participation in the celebration of a pagan holiday? Once we have known the truth we are supposed to be set free from such bondage.

Paul said to the Galatians: ***"Howbeit then, when ye knew not God, ye did service unto them which by nature are no gods. But now, after that ye have known God, or rather are known of God, how turn ye again to the weak and beggarly elements, whereunto ye desire again to be in bondage? Ye observe days, and months, and times, and years. I am afraid of you, lest I have bestowed upon you labour in vain." (Galatians 4:8-11)***

The holidays and seasons which have been so falsely associated with Christ are not to be celebrated by "true Christians".

Christ gave us instructions very clearly concerning how to do service, or worship him. He said, ***"God is a spirit: and they that worship him must worship in spirit and in truth." (John 4:24)***

Again he said, ***"If ye love me, keep my commandments." (John 14-15)*** He summed up his commandments very plainly when he said,***"The first of all the commandments is; Hear, O Israel; The Lord our God is one Lord: and thou shalt love the Lord thy God with all thy heart, and with all thy soul, and with all thy mind, and with all thy strength: this is the first commandment. And the second is like, namely this, Thou shalt love thy neighbor as thyself. There is none other commandment greater than these." (Mark 12:29-31)***

If we truly worship him according to these commandments and show our love to him continually, what is there left in us to celebrate or show more love during a particular time or season of the year? If we can muster up more love for him during the Christmas season, this only means we do not love him with all our soul, heart, mind and strength during the rest of the year.

With this truth, we can only determine that Christ was never in Christmas! Traditions of man have put him there against his will. Those that celebrate Christmas would do well to hear what Jesus said to the Scribes and Pharisees: ***"Thus have ye made the commandment of God of none effect by your tradition." (Matthew 15:6)*** Again Paul said to the church of Colosse: ***"Beware lest any man spoil you through philosophy and vain deceit, after the tradition of men, after the rudiments of the world and not after Christ." (Colossians 2:8)***

The Festival of the Assumption which is held on August 15 is in celebration to the divinity of Mary, the mother of Jesus. It is proclaimed that she was ascended into Heaven and is divine as the

"Mother of God". There is absolutely no basis for this in scripture. The source, however, can be found in Paganism. All Pagan doctrines attribute divinity to the mother of their God and contend she was ascended to heaven.

The very first verse in the Holy Scriptures states, ***"In the beginning God created the heaven and the earth." (Genesis 1:1)***

How then could Mary be the mother of God, when there is only one God. God, himself declared, ***"Ye are my witnesses, saith the Lord, and my servant whom I have chosen; that ye may know and believe me, and understand that I am he: before me there was no God formed, neither shall there be after me. I, even I, am the Lord; and beside me there is no saviour." (Isaiah 43:10-11)***

Halloween is another Pagan holiday that has crept into the realm of false Christianity, and is even celebrated in the church ceremonies. This requires no effort to find the source of these abominable practices. It is a well known fact that the origin of Halloween is the worship of Satan and satanic beings. How then could a serious Christian follow such practices?

One of the most amazing discrepancies in the form of Christian worship in many churches today is prayer. Prayer is man's method of communication with God, and established the basis for his interpersonal relationship with the God he serves. Prayer is defined as "reverent entreaty to a divine being" closely associated with supplication, which is "humble entreaty". The purpose of prayer is to convey to ones God your personal recognition, adoration, belief, confession, petition, and thanksgiving. According to the teachings of Christ and his apostles, this act of communication resulted in immeasurable benefits to the sincere practitioner.

A study of the scriptures will show that prayer is the most

predominate act of worship one can undertake. The results of prayer to God are likened to the communications of a child to his father, a servant to his master, a creature to his creator, and the guilty to his accuser and judge. The examples presented throughout the scriptures present an intelligent intercourse with the omnipotent God of all power. In light of these many and varied examples of prayer, it would seem reasonable to assume one should make every attempt to pray with complete coherence and reasonable intellect.

Prayers in many of today's churches have been relegated to forms and senseless repetition and are presented in the primitive method of the pagan worshippers. Christ, himself warned us against these abominable practices, indicating prayers of this type would not only be sinful but be labour in vain. He not only admonished us but he gave us an acceptable example of a proper prayer, one which could result in the intended desire. He said, ***"And when thou prayest, thou shalt not be as the hypocrites are: for they love to pray standing in the synagogues*** (churches) ***and in the corners of the streets*** (public), ***that they may be seen of men. Verily I say unto you, they have their reward. But thou, when thou prayest, enter into thy closet, and when thou hast shut thy door, pray to thy Father which is in secret; and thy Father which seeth in secret shall reward thee openly. But when ye pray, use not vain repetitions, as the heathen do: for they think they shall be heard for their much speaking. Be not ye therefore like unto them: for your Father knoweth what things ye have need of, before ye ask him."***

***"After this 'manner' therefore pray ye: Our Father which art in heaven, Hallowed be thy name. Thy kingdom come. Thy will be done in earth, as it is in heaven. Give us this day our daily bread. And forgive us our debts, as we forgive our***

***debtors. And lead us not into temptation, but deliver us from evil: For thine is the kingdom, and the power, and the glory, forever, Amen." (Matthew 6:5-13)***

Notice he very clearly stated this was only an example when he said, ***"After this 'manner' therefore pray ye"***. He did not intend this sample prayer to be instituted as an impersonal repetitive ritual as has become so common among Christian churches of today. Repetitive use of this prayer is contrary to his own words of "use not vain repetitions". To understand the senselessness of this type of repetitive entreaty, one needs only imagine his own child confronting him daily with a repetitive communication presented in the form of a ritual. How can one expect such a prayer to be answered.

These words of Christ show complete rejection to any prayers that are memorized or repetitive in nature. Isaiah stated God's rejection of this form of worship when he said concerning the Children of Israel, ***"Wherefore the Lord said, Forasmuch as this people draw near me with their mouth, and with their lips do honour me, but have removed their heart far from me, and their fear toward me is taught by the precept of men: Therefore, behold, I will proceed to do a marvelous work among this people, even a marvelous work and a wonder: for the wisdom of their wise men shall perish, and the understanding of their prudent men shall be hid." (Isaiah 29:13-14)***

There is absolutely no scriptural basis for the use of beads, such as the Rosary to keep count of the vain repetitive prayers of modern Catholicism. A study of paganistic worship will uncover the origin of the prayer beads to be found in the heathenistic customs which God proclaimed as abominations to him. However man has instituted this abominable practice into Christian worship against the will of the "never changing God".

The practice of praying to those which have been decreed saints by the acts of man is also contrary to the words of Christ which have been previously stated. Christ's statement concerning prayer was limited to prayer to the Father. He said, ***"Pray to thy father".*** There are no scriptures which condone praying to any but God the Father. The very definition of prayer or "reverent" entreaty, is an act of worship. According to the scriptural account, it would be to no avail to pray to any saint and expect him or her to act as an intercessor to God for us. Apostle Paul told Timothy, ***"For there is one God, and one mediator between God and men, the man Christ Jesus." (I Timothy 2:5)***

The depth of Paganism in the churches goes even into the structure of the church building. The Catholic Church followed the Roman pagan temple structure in the beginning. They carried over into their form of Christianity all the attributes of image worship which was previously so great a part of Paganism. Even today, the Catholic Churches are resplendent with statues and finery, while the comfort for the lay people leaves much to be desired. Nudity in the Catholic Churches, among the images and paintings, is prevalent everywhere. God considers nakedness as private and personal; and he does not condone public show of nakedness.

The church structure evolved into the cottage structure with a steeple. For a long time, a church without a steeple appeared to be incomplete. What most "Christians" don't know is that the church steeple spire evolved directly representing the Phallic symbol of pagan sexual worship. The phallic symbol is the representative of the erect male organ.

***"And the Lord spake unto Moses, saying, Speak unto the children of Israel, and say unto them, I am the Lord your God.***

***After the doings of the land of Egypt, wherein ye dwelt, shall ye not do: and after the doings of the land of Canaan, whither I bring you, shall ye not do: neither shall ye walk in their ordinances.***

***Ye shall do my judgments, and keep mine ordinances, to walk therein: I am the Lord your God. Ye shall therefore keep my statues, and my judgments: which if a man do, he shall live in them: I am the Lord." (Leviticus 18:1-5)***

God never condoned the practice of copying the traditions and customs of the heathen to be worshipped in the name of Christ. He still considers these acts as an abomination, and worthy of his contempt.

# THEOLOGY

***"But the natural man receiveth not the things of the Spirit of God: for they are foolishness unto him: neither can he know them, because they are spiritually discerned."***

***I Corinthians 2:14***

Theology is a philosophy of religion. Theology incorporates the study of God and his relation to man and the world. To accomplish this study, the theologian must resort to the limited knowledge of the mortal man. In an attempt to understand the incomprehensible infinity of God, mere mortal man becomes embroiled in confusion and contradictions.

The theologian resorts to the basis of his knowledge, (the historical philosophers). Their doctrines were theories conceived within the limited confines of their mere mortal minds. Some of the philosophers most respected, by the theologian are: Pythagoras (570 - 500 BC), Socrates (469 - 399 BC), Plato (427 - 347 BC) and Aristotle (384 - 322 BC).

None of these sources of intellect claimed personal knowledge of God through communication and or revelation. Their theories of God, the universe, life, and reality depended entirely upon the conclusions of their mortal minds. As a result, they can only be classified as unbelievers. Although none of these mental greats had any personal experience with God, they became the source of knowledge for many of the so-called "Church Fathers" and the subsequent theologians.

Each successive philosophy tends to accept at least part of

the doctrines propounded by his predecessor. Upon this base, he adds his opinions and views. More validity is accredited to these self-styled philosophers and their modern disciples, than is attributed to the inspired Word of God, presented to man through divine revelations. Man tends to discount divine revelation as too mystical for acceptance. Man's general attitude is: it must come from man's mind to be acceptable.

The theologian relies on the premise that all accounts of scriptures must be logical to be accepted as valid. The word logical means: that which agrees with accepted principles of logic. The word logic means: that which can be demonstrated in accordance to reason, reason being limited to mans knowledge and experience. The words, accepted principles are the key to the misuse of this premise based on what is logical. What is more logical than actual results whether they can be reasoned logical or not? Facts of actuality speak for themselves.

The theologian feels a need to rationalize the Word of God. He deems it necessary to substitute a natural logical reason to replace a supernatural explanation. Through his superior intelligence, he attempts to present the inspired Word of God in a more believable form. Thus, he proves his own unbelief, by this rationalization. He cannot accept God's Word at face value. As mere man he exalts himself above God and his inspired prophets. He declares, by his actions, that he knows better than God how to present his message to man.

No wonder Paul said, ***"For I say, through the grace given unto me, to every man that is among you, not to think of himself more highly than he ought to think; but to think soberly, according as God hath dealt to every man the measure of faith." (Romans 12:3)*** No wonder there exists such a diversity of contradictions among the various proponents of theology. No wonder it is popular to question the validity of the Bible and its origin.

God's Word should not be questioned any more than the existence of the universe should be questioned. As the scientist explores, tests, and discovers the unknown mysteries of creation, the theologian should explore, test, and discover the truth of God's Word. Does not man's own wisdom proclaim, "experience is the best teacher." The words of the prophet Agur declares, ***"Every word of God is pure: he is a shield unto them that put their trust in him. Add thou not unto His words, lest he reproves thee, and thou be found a liar." (Proverbs 30:5-6)***

The early theologians, generally referred to as, "The Church Fathers", relied very heavily upon the intellect of the ancient philosophers for their interpretations of scripture. It is not the attempt here to question the sincerity, devotion, or honesty of these devout men nor of the present day theologians. It must be pointed out however, that to rationalize or even to reword the proclamations of God can only result in dilution and loss of divine effect. This, then causes misinterpretations, and leads to confusion and contradictions. God's Word can only be interpreted by God's Word, or should it be said, "Scripture should be interpreted by scripture."

Paul said, ***"God is not the author of confusion, but of peace, as in all churches of the saints." (I Corinthians 14:33)*** He told the Corinthians, ***"Now I beseech you, brethren, by the name of our Lord Jesus Christ, that ye all speak the same thing, and that there be no divisions among you; but that ye be perfectly joined together in the same mind and in the same judgment." (I Corinthians 1:10)***

He further declared, *"For it is written, I will destroy the wisdom of the wise, and will bring to nothing the understanding of the prudent. Where is the wise? Where is the scribe? Where is the disputer of this world? Hath not God made foolish the wisdom of this world? For after that in the wisdom of God the world by wisdom knew not God, it pleased God by the foolishness of preaching to save them that believe." (I Corinthians 1:19-21)*

He set himself as an example when he told them, *"And I, brethren, when I came to you, came not with excellency of speech or of wisdom, declaring unto you the testimony of God. For I determined not to know any thing among you, save Jesus Christ, and him crucified. And I was with you in weakness, and in fear, and in much trembling. And my speech and my preaching was not with enticing words of man's wisdom, but in demonstration of the Spirit and of power: that your faith should not stand in the wisdom of men, but in the power of God.*

*Howbeit we speak wisdom among them that are perfect: yet not the wisdom of this world, nor of the princes of this world, that come to nought: But we speak the wisdom of God in a mystery, even the hidden wisdom, which God ordained before the world unto our glory: which none of the princes of this world knew: for had they known it, they would not have crucified the Lord of glory.*

*But as it is written, Eye hath not seen, nor ear heard, neither have entered into the heart of man, the things which God hath prepared for them that love him. But God hath revealed them unto us by his Spirit: for the Spirit searcheth all things, yea the deep things of God.*

***For what man knoweth the things of a man, save the spirit of man which is in him? even so the things of God knoweth no man, but the spirit of God. Now we have received, not the spirit of the world, but the spirit which is of God; that we might know the things that are freely given to us of God. Which things also we speak, not in the words which man's wisdom teacheth, but which the Holy Ghost teacheth; comparing spiritual things with spiritual. But the natural man receiveth not the things of the Spirit of God: for they are foolishness unto him: neither can he know them, because they are spiritually discerned. But he that is spiritual judgeth all things, yet he himself is judged of no man. For who hath known the mind of the Lord, that he may instruct him? But we have the mind of Christ." (I Corinthians 2:1-16)***

Apostle Paul, a devout man, a Pharisee, the son of a Pharisee, a highly educated man who sat at the feet of Gamaliel, stripped himself of mans wisdom and professed to know only the scriptures, "as it is written." He did not resort to rationalization of the scriptures but accepted them at face value. He and the rest of the apostles of the New Testament taught the scriptures as they were written and made no attempt to Theologize them.

He left a perpetual warning to the would be theologian when he said, ***"Let no man deceive himself. If any man among you seemeth to be wise in this world, let him become a fool, that he may be wise. For the wisdom of this world is foolishness with God. For it is written, 'he taketh the wise in their own craftiness'. And again, 'The Lord knoweth the thoughts of the wise, that they are vain." (I Corinthians 3:18-20)***

Thus, we see self esteem and the wisdom of this world is the very foundation of Theology. Therefore, Theology is unveiled as the seed of apostasy. The searcher for truth finds this truth: "As man increases in the rationalization of the scriptures according to the vanity of his mind, so increases the heretical divisions among those who would call themselves Christian."

Christ set the example of servitude to his fellow man. Apostle Peter exhorted the church leaders, ***"Feed the flock of God which is among you, taking the oversight thereof, not by constraint, but willingly; not for filthy lucre, but of a ready mind. Neither as being lords over God's heritage, but being examples to the flock." (I Peter 5:2-3)*** Yet, it is found the "Church Fathers" of today's Christianity embarking on a policy contrary of these principles established by Christ and his Apostles.

The writings of the early fathers reveal a policy of constraint and domination by those in authority over the lay members of the congregation. What was a family of believers, became in time a congregation under strict rule of a single bishop. This policy cannot be substantiated in the teachings of Christ nor in the writings of the Apostles.

This influx of non-Christians into the congregations of true believers became apparent before the end of the Apostle's Era. Jude informed the true Christians, the church had already strayed from its initial principles of doctrine. He wrote, ***"Beloved, when I gave all diligence to write unto you of the common salvation, it was needful for me to write unto you, and exhort you that ye should earnestly contend for the faith which was once delivered unto the saints.***

***For there are certain men crept in unawares, who were before of old ordained to this condemnation, ungodly men, turning the grace of our God into lasciviousness, and denying the only Lord God, and our Lord Jesus Christ." (Jude 3-7)*** He continued, ***"Likewise also these filthy dreamers defile the flesh, despise dominion, and speak evil of dignities." (Jude 8)***

***"But these speak evil of those things which they know not: but what they know naturally, as brute beasts, in those things they corrupt themselves. Woe unto them! for they have gone in the way of Cain, and ran greedily after the error of Balaam for reward, and perished in the gainsaying of Core. These are spots in your feasts of charity, when they feast with you, feeding themselves without fear: clouds they are without water, carried about of winds; trees whose fruit withereth, without fruit, twice dead, plucked up by the roots; Raging waves of the sea, foaming out their own shame; wandering stars, to whom is reserved the blackness of darkness for ever." (Jude 10-13)***

***"These are murmurers, complainers, walking after their own lusts; and their mouth speaketh great swelling words, having men's persons in admiration because of advantage." (Jude 16)***

This undesirable element within the church proceeded, through devious means, to assume authority over the innocent members of the various congregations. This became apparent by the deviations from Christ's teachings in the doctrines being taught in the fourth century. The true Christians, which chose to adhere strictly to the teachings of Christ and his Apostles, were castigated and subdued. They were removed from the church and labeled as heretical cults. The ever increasing Apostate Church flourished and sought worldly acclaim as "The Church" with Christ as its founder. The "True Christian" faded into obscurity due to his unpopular strict adherence to the teachings of Christ and His Apostles and their doctrine of self denial.

The Apostate Church became the ravenous wolf in sheep's clothing which Christ warned of. All Christians, both apostate and true, were found to be the target of much persecution. Many innocent victims were martyred while clinging to the false doctrines and traditions of men instead of being true Christians, following the teachings of Christ and his apostles. The situation still stands today. Many well meaning would-be Christians are blindly following the dictates of Theology and not Christ.

Paul warned, ***"Beware lest any man spoil you through philosophy and vain deceit, after the tradition of men, after the rudiments of the world, and not after Christ." (Colossians 2:8)***

# TRADITIONS AND CUSTOMS

***"And he said unto them, Full well ye reject the commandment of God, that ye may keep your own tradition."***
***Mark 7:9***

Throughout the Western world people have become "Christians", not by conviction, not by personal belief, not as a way of salvation for their soul, but as a way of life to comply with the social pressures of our time. Anyone who does not proclaim himself a Christian is labeled an outcast and rejected by today's society. Man generally accepts Christianity, not as a way to please his creator, but rather to find acceptance among his neighbors. As a result, the churches of today are found to be Christian in name only.

A review of the customs and traditions of the so called Christian Churches of today will expose where they deviate from the doctrine of Christ and the teachings of the apostles. It will also show specifically how they have been duped into being a victim as well as partaker in this crime against humanity.

The major activities in today's churches are dealing with community problems and considerations rather than salvation for the individual soul. It would appear Salvation of the soul has become old fashioned and out of style. One finds activities such as Boy Scouts, Girl Scouts, dances, parties, youth recreation, building programs, and even politics occupying the majority of the effort in what was intended to be the house of prayer.

The New Testament church was established by the apostles and founded by Christ with himself as the head. They laid the ground work for our church of today. We are told by the most devout of today's Christians that the Church Christ founded cannot exist in today's society. How can such a mutinous group of ardent Christians expect to succeed in their attempt to overthrow the lord and saviour of all mankind? Do they not believe him when he said, ***"All power is given unto me in heaven and earth?" (Matthew 28:18)***

Why has it become necessary for his house of prayer to become the investor and founder of "Big Business"? Did he ever lead us to believe we had time to concern ourselves with such a wicked endeavor as seeking riches? To the contrary, he taught that, ***"It is easier for a camel to go through the eye of a needle, than for a rich man to enter into the kingdom of God." (Matthew 19:24)*** Solomon said, ***"There is that maketh himself rich, yet hath nothing: there is that maketh himself poor, yet hath great riches." (Proverbs 13:7)***

We find the Christian Churches of today setting the example for the laity to pursue riches and treasures on earth. While the Church itself is the leader in practicing materialism, it is small wonder the lay member finds it permissible to put all he has into seeking greater riches. As a matter of fact, more often than not, the Church leaders are encouraging their members to constantly improve their standard of living, thus increasing the "take" in the offering plate.

The members are even coerced into signing a pledge when they do not have enough money immediately available for certain contributions solicited by the Church. As a result, many find themselves honor bound to pay off this debt made under duress. Many are pressured to give above and beyond their reasonable capability. Forgotten are the words of Apostle Paul to the

Corinthians, ***"Now therefore perform the doing of it; that as there was a readiness to will, so there may be a performance also out of that which ye have. For if there be first a willing mind, it is accepted according that a man hath, and not according to that he hath not." (II Corinthians 8:11-12)*** He spoke this concerning contributions in church and was very clear in his instructions that none should give more than he had, or was willing to give.

The New Testament Church, which was meant to be the example and the foundation for today's church was established on the principle of donations not collections. The early church flourished financially due to the unselfish donations of its members. All that would be "true Christians" followed the teachings of Christ and exercised their new found faith and sold all that they had, donating the entire proceeds to the church. Thus, their faith was established and all that believed were together, and had all things common. ***"And the multitude of them that believed were of one heart and of one soul: neither said any of them that ought of the things which he possessed was his own; but they had all things common. And with great power gave the apostles witness of the resurrection of the Lord Jesus: and great grace was upon them all. Neither was there any among them that lacked: for as many as were possessors of lands or houses sold them, and brought the prices of the things that were sold, And laid them down at the apostles feet: and distribution was made unto every man according as he had need." (Acts 5:32-35)***

This was the common salvation and the faith referred to by Jude when he wrote, ***"Beloved, when I gave diligence to write unto you of the common salvation, it was needful for me to write unto you, and exhort you that ye should earnestly contend***

***for the faith which was once delivered unto the saints." (Jude 3)*** At the time of this writing, the church had already begun to stray from the principles upon which it was founded, thus prompting Jude to give them stern warning. As an example he said, ***"And the angels which kept not their first estate, but left their own habitation, he hath reserved in everlasting chains under darkness unto the judgment of the great day." (Jude 6)***

Christ taught, the righteous shall live by faith with a total dependence on God. If the churches of today would teach this doctrine and practice the love of God, (which surpasseth all knowledge) there would be no need for the churches to be involved in "Big Business". The truth is evident. The very churches which proclaim his doctrine do not practice his teachings. Christ himself declared God would provide all our needs without us taking thought for tomorrow. The Christian Churches of today, do not have enough belief in the God they profess to worship to live by faith as Christ intended. All who do not live by faith are not just. All who are not just are not Christian, but are in the process of deceiving or being deceived if they claim to be Christians.

Nevertheless, Church has become big business in today's society. It is not uncommon to find large church organizations as owners of Insurance Companies. Some of these Insurance Companies even carry the name of "Christian". What a paradox this is, to the teachings of Christ. He said, ***"Take no thought for your life, what ye shall eat, or what ye shall drink; nor yet for your body, what ye shall put on. Is not life more than meat, and the body than raiment?" (Matthew 6:25)***

Although many persons claim Christ as their leader and profess to believe in his teachings, few will accept this as a way of life for themselves. For a person not to take thought for the future, not to provide a nest egg of savings for old age, is unacceptable in this so called "Christian" Civilization. It is hard to conceive why people will even accept the name of Christian, when his teachings are so foreign to the modern way of life. Christ himself said, ***"Whosoever therefore shall deny me before men, him will I also deny before my Father which is in heaven." (Matthew 10:33)*** It would appear, though many confess to "accept Jesus Christ as their personal saviour," in reality they have denied him and he has rejected them. How then can so many claim to be his followers when he refuses to be their leader?

Many of the churches have founded hospitals to care for the sick and provide a place for their convalescence. Christ sent out his disciples and commanded them to heal the sick. It is hard to conceive of Christ condoning multitudes of sick and lame remaining in misery while man uses his own ingenuity and guess work to relieve them. Christ, himself, set the example, by healing all manner of diseases and afflictions without the aid of medicine or treatment. He left us with this assurance, ***"Verily, verily, I say unto you, He that believeth on me, the works that I do shall he do also; and greater works than these shall he do." (John 14:12)*** The Christian of today claims to believe in the resurrection of Christ and proclaims once a year that "He Lives". They also entertain the hope, that although life in the natural body will cease, they will one day, in like manner, be resurrected to meet him. How can a person subscribe to such a magnificent power of God and yet deny he has the ability to heal our physical ailments. He himself left no doubt to those that would believe his words, he would heal their bodies and forgive their sins.

Today's Christian, that puts his hope and trust in man, is deserving of the admonishment Paul made concerning Israel. He said, ***"For I bear them record that they have a zeal of God, but not according to knowledge. For they being ignorant of God's righteousness, and going about to establish their own righteousness, have not submitted themselves unto the righteousness of God." (Acts 10:2-3)*** He referred to these modern Christians saying, ***"They have a form of godliness, but denying the power thereof: from such turn away." (II Timothy 3:5)***

It would appear to the observer of today's church services that more effort is placed upon the entertainment and satisfaction of the individuals natural desires, than the fulfillment of his spiritual need. Some have even endorsed the doctrine: that to satisfy mans physical desires is to discharge his spiritual requirements. This doctrine is the basis of the belief of some, which infers, as long as a person enjoys himself in this life he is fulfilling the purpose of his creation and pleasing his creator. It is a peculiar thing that a Christian could maintain this view when Christ so plainly stated. ***"If any man will come after me, let him deny himself, and take up his cross and follow me." (Luke 9:23)*** Apostle John commanded: ***"Love not the world, neither the things that are in the world, if any man love the world, the love of the Father is not in him. For all that is in the world, the lust of the flesh, and the lust of the eyes is not of the Father, but is of the world. And the world passeth away; and the lust thereof: but he that doeth the will of God abideth forever." (I John 2:15-17)***

The churches today, as well as this materialistic society we live in, is motivated exclusively by pride. The primary concept of advertising in today's business world appeals to the pride of the individual. We are constantly reminded that pride should be one of our most cherished characteristics. We are taught to have pride in our family, our home, our community, our country, even our church building. The result of this pride-motivated society, is to make us self-centered and egotistical concerning anything that we are personally associated with. We have thus become extremely competitive and envious with our neighbor and fellow man. Is this the doctrine which Christ taught?

Solomon wrote in his proverbs of wisdom, ***"When pride cometh, then cometh shame, but with the lowly is wisdom," (Proverbs 11:2)*** and ***"Pride goeth before destruction, and a haughty spirit before a fall." (Proverbs 16:18)*** He also wrote, ***"A man's pride shall bring him low: but honour shall uphold the humble in spirit." (Proverbs 29:23)*** Christ aptly warned us, ***"That which cometh out of the man, that defileth the man. For from within, out of the heart of men, proceed evil thoughts, adulteries, fornications, murders, thefts, covetousness, wickedness, deceit, lasciviousness, an evil eye, blasphemy, pride, and foolishness: all these evil things come from within, and defile the man." (Mark 7:20-23)***

Surely a person cannot be defiled, and still profess to be a Christian, a true follower of Christ. Paul exhorted the Romans and all that would be a follower of Christ when he said, ***"I beseech ye therefore, brethren, by the mercies of God, that ye present your bodies a living sacrifice, holy, acceptable unto God, which is your reasonable service. And be not conformed to this world: but be ye transformed by the renewing of your mind, that ye may prove what is that good, and acceptable, and perfect will of God." (Romans 12:1-2)***

The methods and customs of worship in today's churches of Christianity are as varied as their names and different doctrines imply. It would appear the teachers of Christianity found Christ their leader and his apostles completely incompetent in their instructions. They found it necessary to institute their own forms of worship which obviously they felt were superior to any which were left them by Christ or his personally appointed apostles. Many of the customs of worship we find today, have virtually no foundation in the scriptures. In many cases, the teachings of Christ and his apostles actually forbid some of the customs practiced in the worship service of today's Christian churches.

As we continue to review some of these modern customs of worship, we will discover they are based upon the traditions of our fathers rather than the Biblical record of Christ's own words and precepts of his Apostles. Man has voluntarily chosen his own way of life and therefore, ***"All we like sheep have gone astray; we have turned everyone to his own way;" (Isaiah 53:6)*** All would be Christians should ask themselves, "Am I worshipping according to truth or tradition"? We should all be aware that there are even churches that assign a higher order of precedence to tradition than to the teachings of Christ.

# CHURCH GOVERNMENT

*"And when the ten heard it, they began to be much displeased with James and John. But Jesus called them to him, and saith unto them, Ye know that they which are accounted to rule over the Gentiles exercise lordship over them; and their great ones exercise authority upon them. But so shall it not be among you: but whosoever will be great among you, shall be your minister: and whosoever of you will be the chiefest, shall be servant of all..."*

*Mark 10:41-44*

King Solomon in his wisdom, observed, *"God hath made man upright; But they have sought out many inventions." (Ecclesiastes 7:29)* According to the Biblical record, the very days in the existence of man found mankind pursuing life contrary to the desires of God. This waywardness of man reached such proportions, that God deemed it necessary to destroy man from the face of the earth. *"And God saw that the wickedness of man was great in the earth, and that every imagination of the thoughts of his heart was only evil continually. And it repented the LORD that he had made man on the earth, and it grieved him at his heart. And the LORD said, I will destroy man whom I have created from the face of the earth; both man, and beast, and the creeping thing, and the fowls of the air; for it repenteth me that I have made them." (Genesis 6:5-7)*

Down through the ages, man has continued to stray from the

will and purpose of his Creator and has sought to live according to his own desires. Man has chosen to reject the wishes and instructions of his Maker and establish rules and regulations more suitable to his liking.

Christ gave definite instructions or rather commandments concerning the proper behavior and relationship, which should be adhered to, in man's association with his fellow man. Subsequently, those claiming to be disciples of Christ have again chosen to reject the teachings of Christ and the examples of the apostles. Christianity, today, is engulfed in a multitude of organizations, denominations, cults, and sects. Each group has established its own peculiar form of government. The rules and regulations of various forms of church governments are adapted to suit the desires and peculiarities of the founders of the group. Many times a particular church government has become an adopted variation of an already existing church group. A close study will show that very little attention, if any, has been given to the teachings of Christ in the establishment of most church governments.

In all of his teachings, Jesus Christ was opposed to any one man exalting himself above another in any way. He said, ***"For whosoever exalteth himself shall be abased; and he that humbleth himself shall be exalted." (Luke 14:11)*** His second commandment to us meant merely, ***"by love serve one another. For all the law is fulfilled in one word, even in this: Thou shalt love thy neighbor as thy self." (Galatians 5:13-14)*** Paul exhorts us in his letter to the Romans, stating, ***"I beseech you brethren, by the mercies of God, that ye present your bodies a living sacrifice, holy, acceptable unto God, which is your reasonable service. And be not conformed to this world: but be ye transformed by the renewing of your mind, that ye may*** *prove what is that good, and acceptable, and perfect, will of God. For I say through grace given unto me, to every man that is among you, not to think of himself more highly than he ought to think; but to think soberly, according as God hath dealt to every man the measure of faith. For as we have many members in one body and all members have not the same office: So we being many, are one body in Christ and every one members one of another. Having then gifts differing according to the grace that is given to us, whether prophecy, let us prophesy according to the proportion of faith; Or ministry, let us wait on our ministering: or he that teacheth, on teaching; Or he that exhorteth, on exhortation: he that giveth, let him do it with simplicity; he that ruleth, with diligence; he that showeth mercy, with cheerfulness. Let love be without dissimulation* (pretense). *Abhor that which is evil; cleave to that which is good. Be kindly affectioned one to another with brotherly love; in honour preferring one another." (Romans 12:1-10)*

The above establishes that we all have different gifts and the ministry is one of them. The word minister is defined to mean a servant or instrument, of the church. When James and John asked Jesus to *"sit, one on his right hand and one on his left hand, in thy glory", (Mark 10:37)* Jesus rebuked them. When the other apostles heard of the request, they were much displeased with James and John. Jesus saw the spirit of jealousy among the twelve apostles over who would be greatest. *"But Jesus called them to him, and saith unto them, ye know that they which are accounted to rule over the Gentiles, exercise lordship over them; and their great ones exercise authority upon them. But so shall it not be among you: but whosoever will be great*

***among you, shall be your minister*** (servant). ***And whosoever of you will be the chiefest, shall be servant of all. For even the Son of man came not to be ministered unto, but to minister*** (serve) ***and to give his life a ransom for many." (Mark 10:42-45)*** This plainly shows that any church government or organization which exalts one person or office above that of another to exercise lordship or authority is contrary to the Word of God and is not based on New Testament teaching. Church denominations representing Christianity today are greatly divided over the acceptable method of instituting church government within their various organizational hierarchies. Some have accepted the title of Elder for the preaching ministry, while most institute a body of officials disposed organically in ranks and orders, each subordinate to the one above it. This is done in direct contradiction to the instructions of Christ himself.

The office of Bishop is seldom used today in accordance with the instructions so clearly established in the New Testament church. Instead, the title of Bishop is erroneously conferred on an exalted position of authority in the hierarchy of ecclesiastical rulers. Contrary to New Testament example and instruction, some denominational organizations do not recognize nor institute the office of Bishop in their form of church government. Instead, they institute some other title or office such as President, Vice-President, Reverend, Pastor, Assistant Pastor,..etc., in various levels of authority. In many of these groups, the qualifications of the preaching ministry as established by the apostles is completely ignored.

The existence of the hierarchy of government is a carry over of the so-called apostates from the Roman Catholic church. Protestantism has instituted a hierarchal form of church government patterned generally in one form or another after their "Mother Church".

A cursory study of Paganism, which existed many centuries before the foundation of the Roman Catholic Church, will reveal this to be the origin of hierarchal church government.

With a clear understanding of the above, we can get a deeper insight into Apostle Paul's writing to the Ephesians concerning the ministry. He states, ***"But unto every one of us is given grace according to the measure of the gift of Christ. Wherefore he saith, when he ascended up on high, he led captivity captive, and gave gifts unto men." (Ephesians 4:7-8)*** He continues: ***"And he gave some apostles; and some, prophets; and some, evangelists; and some pastors and teachers; for the perfecting of the saints, for the work of the ministry, for the edifying of the body of Christ*** (the Church)." ***(Ephesians 4:11-12) "So we, being many, are one body in Christ, and every one members one of another." (Romans 12:5)***

So we see the five-fold ministry (as it is often referred to), is not made up of five different offices of the church which is generally taught, but rather different gifts or functions of the ministry, required for the perfecting of the saints.

There are only two offices of the ministry in the New Testament, and they are Bishop and Deacon. The office of Bishop was filled by elders which were ordained into this position by the apostles which received their authority by the grace given them by the gift of apostle.

The term Pastor is given today to the leader or head of a local church congregation. The practice of one man rule or leader in a local church congregation is not founded on the examples set forth in the New Testament church, rather this practice was adopted from the Catholic form of church government instituting a priest over a local parish or congregation. This tradition emanated from Paganism.

The word "pastors" is mentioned only once in the New Testament. It has already been established this is only one of the spiritual gifts of the ministry and there is no reference found where this is the title of the head or ruler of a local congregation in the early church. Careful study will show there is only one head of "The Church" and that is Jesus Christ.

The word pastor in the New Testament comes from the Greek word "Poimen" meaning "to feed" or shepherd. The New Testament teaches that elders of a local congregation are charged with the responsibility to feed (pastor) the flock of God, taking the oversight thereof. The Old Testament was translated from Hebrew while the New Testament was translated from Greek. It is easy to see how one English word (pastor) could be translated with different connotations from two different languages, and still have the same basic meaning. Pastor in the Old Testament is Shepherd or flock feeder while the New Testament meaning is one who has the ability or gift to feed the flock.

As previously mentioned, those charged with the responsibility of feeding the flock in each local congregation were "the elders which are among you". During the days of the early church, there was only one local church or congregation in each city and there were elders ordained to the office of Bishop in every city. Thus the responsibility of feeding the flock and ruling a local congregation belongs to this group of Ordained Elders, not to a one man ruler or pastor of the congregation. Peter confirms this in his first epistle when he said, ***"The elders which are among you I exhort, who am also an elder, and a witness of the sufferings of***

***Christ, and also partaker of the glory that shall be revealed: Feed the flock of God which is among you, taking the oversight thereof, not by constraint, but willingly; not for filthy lucre, but of a ready mind; Neither as being lords over God's heritage, but being examples to the flock." (I Peter 5:1-3)*** Paul said, ***"Let the elders that rule well be counted worthy of the double honour, especially they who labour in the word and doctrine." (I Timothy 5:17)*** This is further proven by the fact that Luke, Paul, Peter, James, nor John, ever once mentioned the one man head or ruler of a local church in all the writings of the New Testament.

One man rule in a local congregation has a tendency to cause this person to be exalted above what is expected of a true disciple of Christ. The very position of authority, the luxury of the pulpit, with the special seats for ministers, breeds self conceit as well as inviting the congregation to worship their pastor who is in reality encroaching on and detracting from the Glory of the True Pastor and High Priest, Jesus Christ.

There are references to two groups in the preaching ministry of the New Testament. These are referred to as apostles and elders. Being ministers of the Gospel, these are all qualified for the office of Bishop. The distinction is made to indicate a difference in their ministerial calling. An apostle is an elder, according to the above reference of Peter, which has received the spiritual gift of apostle with power and authority to ordain other elders, and thus establish local churches as well as preach the gospel as a traveling evangelist.

These were the instructions of Paul to Titus when he wrote: ***"For this cause left I thee in Crete, that thou shouldest set in order the things that are wanting, and ordain elders in every city, as I had appointed thee: If any be blameless, the husband of one wife, having faithful children not accused of riot or***

***unruly. For a bishop must be blameless, as the steward of God; not given to wine, no striker, not given to filthy lucre; But a lover of hospitality, a lover of good men, sober, just, holy, temperate; Holding fast the faithful word as he hath been taught, that he may be able by sound doctrine both to exhort and to convince the gainsayers." (Titus 1:5-9)*** The record of the Acts of the Apostles includes the following passage: ***"And when they had preached the gospel to that city, and had taught many, they returned again to Lystra, and to Iconium, and Antioch, Confirming the souls of the disciples, and exhorting them to continue in the faith and that we must through much tribulation enter into the kingdom of God. And when they had ordained them elders in every church, and had prayed with fasting, they commended them to the Lord, on whom they believed." (Acts 14:21-23)***

It goes without saying to fulfill this calling, an apostle must also be endowed with the gift of knowledge, wisdom and healing to work the signs of an apostle. This does not mean to say that an apostle is not an elder. It would establish rather that an apostle is an elder endowed with special abilities or gifts compared to those of other elders. That an apostle is also an elder, is very well established in the scriptures. As mentioned above, Peter refers to himself as an elder, while the Apostle John refers to himself as an elder in the first verses of II John and III John.

The word "elder" has a dual meaning in the scriptures, although both stem from the same basic definition. Again, remember the Old Testament was translated from Hebrew while the New Testament was translated from Greek. This would account for the slightly different connotations of use of the word "elder" in the Old and New Testaments.

The word "elder" in the Old Testament pertains to the older members of the tribes of Israel and the aged head of a family. The elders of the Old Testament represented their people and exercised rule and authority over them.

The word "elder" in the New Testament comes from the Greek word "presbuteros", the same source as the word presbytery. Elder in the New Testament Church is used interchangeable with the word Bishop and refers to the person which is an office holder in the church.

A thorough study of the New Testament writings including Christ's teachings, show the practice of instituting a pastor as the head of a local church congregation is not Biblical but rather is a result of traditions of men and originates from the paganistic form of worship. Paul very clearly warned us, ***"Beware lest any man spoil you through philosophy and vain deceit, after the traditions of men, after rudiments of the world, and not after Christ." (Colossians 2:8)***

It is easy to see the structure of Church Government in the majority of churches claiming to represent Christianity, have no foundation in the Bible. It is reasonable to understand how one could ask, "How can these churches be the true representatives of Christianity, when they reject the teachings of Christ and his apostles as well as the example left us by the New Testament Church."

## APOSTLES' CREED

*"This people draweth nigh unto me with their mouth, and honoureth me with their lips; but their heart is far from me. But in vain they do worship me, teaching for doctrines the commandments of men."*

*(Matthew 15:8-9)*

Much of Christendom has adopted a confession of religious faith or a statement of belief. It has been established that one is a Christian and has fulfilled the requirements of salvation if he believes in all the tenets of this creed. It has been the custom for many centuries to memorize and quote the so-called "Apostles' Creed" as a necessary function of many worship services. It can only be assumed that this practice serves no other purpose than to remind the practitioner of his beliefs. It is certainly reasonable to expect one to confess or acknowledge his beliefs orally whenever the occasion presents itself, but it is hard to conceive the value to be obtained from the ritualistic recital of a creed.

Apostle Paul did say, "If thou shalt confess with thy mouth the Lord Jesus and shalt believe in thine heart that God hath raised him from the dead, thou shalt be saved." Did he mean confess in the form of a ritualistic creed? The biblical record does not substantiate such a custom.

Paul told the Colossians, *"Let the word of Christ dwell in you richly in all wisdom; teaching and admonishing one another in psalms and hymns and spiritual songs, singing with grace in your hearts to the Lord. And whatsoever ye do in word or deed,*

***do all in the name of the Lord Jesus, giving thanks to God and the Father by Him." (Colossians 3:16-17)***

A look into the history of the "Apostles' Creed" becomes very revealing. Until the seventeenth century, Catholics and Protestants alike were taught the creed was written by the apostles on the day of Pentecost. The events of that day are recorded in the second chapter of the Acts of the Apostles. No mention is made to substantiate such a claim. The Roman Catholic Church still holds to this belief according to the current Catholic encyclopedia.

A study of the early church writers, including the biblical record, does not uncover any evidence to support that the apostles formulated, condoned, or practiced, such a ritual. The first writer to record the "Apostles' Creed" was not until the fourth century, A.D. Church history reveals that the "Apostles' Creed" today is not the same one that is purported to be conceived by the apostles. The old Roman Creed, which it is called, was discarded in favor of a revised version. The present form of the "Apostles' Creed" has been in use by the Roman Catholic Church since the seventeenth century. If the old "Roman Creed" was prescribed by the apostles, how could a sincere follower of apostolic teachings accept a forgery, (prepared centuries later), as genuine. The Catholic Encyclopedia, 1907 edition, admits the origin of the "Apostles' Creed" cannot be confirmed. Quote, "we cannot safely affirm the Apostolic composition of the creed."

Since the assumption that the Doctrine of Christ requires the ritualistic use of a creed is baseless in the scriptures, it behooves every would-be Christian to examine more closely what practices are required to establish his belief and acceptance as a true Christian, by Christ.

Christ, himself, made it clear every disciple of his was

required to diligently study the scriptures. One could be his disciple only if he knew the Word of God and lived by it. He said, ***"If ye continue in my word, then are ye my disciples indeed."*** He also told Satan, during his temptation in the wilderness, ***"It is written, Man shall not live by bread alone, but by every word that proceedeth out of the mouth of God." (John 8:31)*** He told the unbelieving Jews to, ***"Search the scriptures; for in them ye think ye have eternal life: and they are they which testify of me." (John 5:39)*** Again, Christ admonished the Sadducees saying to them, ***"Ye do err, not knowing the scriptures, nor the power of God." (Matthew 22:29)***

Christ was especially distraught by the scribes and the Pharisees, which made it a practice to proclaim belief in the scriptures: They prided themselves in their knowledge of the "Word of God". They made a big show of their traditional ritualistic ceremonies, and were devout in the oral affirmation of their belief. Christ denounced them and their practices in this reference to them: ***"This people draweth nigh unto me with their mouth, and honoureth me with their lips; but their heart is far from me. But in vain they do worship me, teaching for doctrines the commandments of men." (Matthew 15:8-9)***

From these statements of Christ, one must perceive that he did not attribute any validity or spiritual value to lip service, such as reciting a Creed as a ritual. He was much more pleased in those who would diligently study and obey the Word of God in the scriptures, and the teachings emanating from his own lips.

The apostles were very outspoken in their instructions concerning the necessity or familiarity and obedience to the scriptures as the prescribed method of affirmation of ones faith in God.

Paul adjured Timothy as a minister of the Gospel of Christ, to, *"Study to show thyself approved unto God, a workman that needeth not to be ashamed, rightly dividing the word of truth." (II Timothy 2:15)* He warned the Romans, *"Be not conformed to this world: but be ye transformed by the renewing of your mind, that ye may prove what is that good and perfect will of God." (Romans 12:2)* In a militant description, he told the Ephesians to, *"Put on the whole armour of God, that ye may be able to stand against the wiles of the devil. (Ephesians 6:11) And take the helmet of salvation, and the sword of the spirit, which is the Word of God." (Ephesians 6:17)*

Peter in writing to the Christians informed them, *"This second epistle, beloved, I now write unto you; in which I stir up your pure minds by way of remembrance: That ye be mindful of the words which were spoken before by the holy prophets, and of the commandment of us the apostles of the Lord and Saviour." (II Peter 3:1-2)* He left the following instruction for all to follow as to the proper method of affirming their belief in Christ, when he said, *"But sanctify the Lord God in your hearts: and be ready always to give an answer to every man that asketh you a reason of the hope that is in you with meekness and fear: Having a good conscience; that whereas they speak evil of you, as of evildoers, they may be ashamed that falsely accuse your good conversation* (conduct) *in Christ." (I Peter 3:15-16)*

Apostle John became the most specific against the practice of doing lip service in affirmation of our love and obedience to Christ. He stated, *"My little children, let us not love in word, neither in tongue; but in deed and in truth." (I John 3:18)* He admonished those who say with their mouths they know Christ but do not practice what they proclaim. He said, ***"And hereby we do know that we know him, if we keep his commandments. He that saith, 'I know him', and keepeth not his commandments, is a liar, and the truth is not in him. But whoso keepeth his word, in him verily is the love of God perfected: hereby know we that we are in him. He that saith he abideth in him ought himself also so to walk, even as he walked." (I John 2:3-6)***

Paul again spoke against those who claim to be Christian in words only, when he said, ***"They profess to know God; but in works they deny him, being abominable, and disobedient, and unto every good work reprobate." (Titus 1:16)***

Thus, it is easy to understand by these statements of Christ and the apostles, that no great consideration is given to the practice of orally proclaiming one's belief in a Creed. This old adage still holds good for a Christian as well as anyone else: "Actions speak louder than words."

Regarding the content of the "Apostles' Creed", a review of each tenet must be examined in light of the scriptural basis for its validity. This is done aside from the consideration of the spiritual value, or lack of it, in the ritualistic recital of a creed.

"I believe in God the Father Almighty, Creator of heaven and earth;"

To believe in God is to believe his Word. As previously stated, Christ admonished Satan with these words, ***"Man shall not live by bread alone, but by every word that proceedeth out of the mouth of God." (Matthew 4:4)*** The proclaimer of this tenet is avowing to accept the validity of God's Words. He also accepts the supremacy of his power without doubting. This acceptance does not come by oral declaration. One can only come to this acceptance by personal experience.

To be able to accept the validity of the Word of God, one must put it to a test. The Psalmist invites all to ***"taste and see that the Lord is good: blessed is the man that trusteth in him." (Psalms 34:8)*** An idea or belief does not become a belief until it is tried and proven. Until the test is made, such an idea as the existence of God is merely an individual's concept. To believe in God is to experience his existence in a real personal way in ones life.

To believe in God is to have faith in him. To believe in God is to please him. The writer to the Hebrews declares, ***"Without faith it is impossible to please him: for he that cometh to God must believe that he is, and that he is a rewarder of them that diligently seek him." (Hebrews 11:6)*** He also said, ***"The just shall live by faith: but if any man draw back my soul shall have no pleasure in him." (Hebrews 10:38)*** You cannot please God without obeying his commandments. You will not obey his commandments until you are familiar with them, and have faith in their validity. This was borne out in Paul's words to the Romans when he said, ***"So then faith cometh by hearing, and hearing by the Word of God." (Romans 10:17)***

The beginning of belief in God is the faith that, God the Father almighty who has power to create heaven and earth also has the power to maintain the accuracy of his word down through the ages including the transition from one language to another. The document or documents claiming to be his word can only be accepted as authentic, when they pass the test of personal experience.

"And in Jesus Christ, his only Son our Lord."

First of all, if the biblical writings are to be accepted as valid, this statement has to be in error. The apostle Luke stated that Adam was a son of God. The writer of Genesis refers to sons of God. Apostle John declares, in reference to Jesus the begotten Son of God, ***"But as many as received him, to them gave he power to become the sons of God, even to them that believe on his name." (John 1:12)***

David, who was approved of Christ, declared to us who the Lord was when he said, ***"Know ye that the Lord he is God: It is he that hath made us, and not we ourselves; we are his people and the sheep of his pasture." (Psalms 100:3)*** Moses wrote, ***"Unto thee it was shown, that thou mightest know that the Lord he is God; there is none else beside him." (Deuteronomy 4:35)*** Christ himself declared, ***"The first of all the commandments is 'Hear, O Israel; The Lord our God is one Lord:' and thou shalt love the Lord thy God with all thine heart, and with all thy soul, and with all thy might." (Deuteronomy 6:4-5)***

To believe the Begotten Son is the second person in the trinity of the Godhead is to believe Christ is a Lord in person aside from God in person. This belief is contradictory to the scriptures cited; establishing the existence of only one Lord. The word "person" in its early definitions applied only to human beings and their personal characteristics. The Bible does not substantiate the teachings of God as a human being separate from the human being of his son Christ. Jesus Christ, the only begotten Son of God informs us that, ***"God is a Spirit" (John 4:24)*** (not a person). Christ described his physical relationship with his father in these words to Philip, ***"He that hath seen me hath seen the Father; and how sayeth thou then, Show us the Father? Believest thou not that I am in the Father, and the Father in me? The words that I***

***speak unto you I speak not of myself: but the Father that dwelleth in me, he doeth the works. Believe me that I am in the Father and the Father in me; or else believe me for the very works' sake." (John 14:9-11)*** He also said, ***"I and my Father are one" (John 10:30)*** (not two persons).

Apostle Paul shed more light on the composition of the Godhead in this statement to the Colossians, ***"For in him*** (Christ) ***dwelleth all the fullness of the Godhead bodily." (Colossians 2:9)*** For the Godhead to be composed of three persons would require three bodies. Apostle Paul said, ***"There is one body, (Christ) and one Spirit (God), even as ye are called in one hope of your calling; One Lord, one faith, one baptism, One God and Father of all, who is above all, and through all and in you all." (Ephesians 4:4-6)***

Apostle John described the Godhead on this wise, ***"In the beginning was the Word, and the Word was with God, and the Word was God." (John 1:1)*** and ***"the Word was made flesh, and dwelt among us, (and we beheld his glory as of the only begotten of the Father,) full of grace and truth." (John 1:14) "He was in the world and the world was made by him, and the world knew him not." (John 1:10)***

Paul became more explicit when he said, ***"And without controversy, great is the mystery of godliness: God was manifest in the flesh, justified in the Spirit, seen of angels, preached unto the Gentiles, believed on in the world, received up into glory." (I Timothy 3:16)*** In light of these scriptures, the fleshly body of the begotten son was the only person of God, which was not a complete singular divine person without the indwelling Spirit of God the Father Almighty. Apostle Paul gave a detailed description of the composition of a complete body (person), in his first letter to the Corinthians. He summed up his description by saying, ***"it is sown a natural body*** (flesh): ***it is raised a spiritual body*** (spirit), ***There is a natural body and there is a spiritual body." (I Corinthians 15:44)***

Thus the existence of the only begotten Son is the physical manifestation of the Word of God dwelling on earth. To believe in Jesus Christ one must believe God the Spirit dwelt on earth in the person of Christ (the flesh of man). To understand the plausibility of God manifesting himself in this manner one need only look into the Old Testament to witness the many varied physical manifestations of God the Spirit, ie. a pillar of fire, a pillar of smoke, a burning bush, a rock, etc.

To believe in Jesus Christ, is to love him, and to love him is to keep his commandments. A person should realize that when he affirms his belief in Christ by reciting the "Apostles' Creed", he is declaring that he is also keeping his commandments. John said, ***"And whatsoever we ask, we receive of him, because we keep his commandments, and do those things that are pleasing in his sight. And this is his commandment, That we should believe on the name of his Son Jesus Christ, and love one another, as he gave us commandment. And he that keepeth his commandments dwelleth in him and he in them. And hereby we know that he abideth in us by the spirit which he hath given us." (I John 3:22-24)*** To believe in Jesus Christ is to be born into the Kingdom of God. Regardless of oral affirmations and claims, one is not a Christian according to the biblical record unless he has entered into the Kingdom of God. Christ told Nicodemus, a ruler of the Jews, ***"Except a man be born of water and of the Spirit, he cannot enter into the Kingdom of God." (John 3:5)*** He further stated, ***"Whosoever believeth that Jesus is the Christ is born of***

*God; and everyone that loveth him that begat, loveth him also that is begotten of him. By this we know that we love God and keep his commandments. For this is the love of God, that we keep his commandments: and his commandments are not grievous. For whatsoever is born of God overcometh the world: and this is the victory that overcometh the world, even our faith." (I John 5:1-4) "We know that whosoever is born of God sinneth not; but he that is begotten of God keepeth himself, and that wicked one toucheth him not. And we know that we are of God, and the whole world lieth in wickedness. And we know that the Son of God is come, and hath given us an understanding, that we may know him that is true, and we are in him that is true, even in his Son Jesus Christ. This is the true God and eternal life." (I John 5:18-20) "If we receive the witness of men, the witness of God is greater: for this is the witness of God which hath testified of his Son. He that believeth on the Son of God hath the witness in himself. He that believeth not God hath made him a liar; because he believeth not the record that God gave of his Son. And this is the record, that God hath given to us eternal life, and this life is in his Son. He that hath the Son hath life; and he that hath not the Son of God hath not life." (I John 5:9-12)*

To summarize; one that states, "I believe in Jesus Christ," is making a declaration that he has attained to a perfect sinless life by keeping all the commandments of God, that he has been born of the water and of the Spirit, that Christ dwells in him, and he in Christ, and he has overcome the world. This is certainly not the condition of a new convert to Christianity.

The final test of ones belief in Jesus Christ is recorded by John in the very words of Christ. *"Verily, verily, I say unto you,*

***He that believeth on me, the works that I do shall he do also; and greater works than these shall he do; because I go unto my Father." (John 14:12)*** It would certainly behoove the proclaimer of the Apostles' Creed to take heed to Paul's warning to the Corinthians when he said, ***"Examine yourselves, whether ye be in the faith; prove your own selves. Know ye not your own selves, how that Jesus Christ is in you except ye be reprobates." (II Corinthians 13:5)***

"Who was conceived by the Holy Ghost."

This tenet is confirmed by scripture, while scripture also declares God is the Father. A question is therefore posed, If the Holy Ghost and God the Father are two different persons in the trinity, how then can they both be the Father? It stands to reason, that which causes a mother to conceive is in fact the father of the begotten. Are we to believe that the person, God, resorted to artificial insemination and caused the person, Holy Ghost, to carry out the act of conception for him?

Would it not be more reasonable to accept that the Holy Ghost was a spiritual manifestation of God the Father which caused Mary to conceive? Thus, completing the act of conception himself, in the form of the Holy Ghost. This would, therefore, account for the validity of the scriptures. Did not God manifest himself in different forms to accomplish various feats throughout the ages? Yet, all these manifestations were in fact God. This remains as proof that there could not be three individual persons in the Godhead.

The logical conclusion that can be substantiated by all the biblical writings is as follows: God the Almighty, which is Spirit, manifested himself in the form of the Holy Ghost to bring to pass the physical creation of the Son of Man in which dwelt the fullness of the Godhead in a bodily form. The begotten Son then was the physical manifestation of God, the Father Almighty in the form of human flesh, with the Holy Spirit of God in him. This is confirmed by Christ's own words when he said, ***"I and my Father are One"*** and, ***"He that hath seen me hath seen the Father"*** and, ***"Believe me that I am in the Father, and the Father in me." (John 14:11)*** This also accounts for the angel's proclamation to Mary, ***"And they shall call his name Emanuel, which being interpreted is 'God with us'." (Matthew 1:23)*** Isaiah's prophecy then comes true. ***"For unto us a child is born, unto us a son is given: and the government shall be on his shoulder: and his name shall be called Wonderful, Counsellor, The mighty God, The everlasting Father, The Prince of Peace." (Isaiah 9:6)***

"I believe in the Holy Ghost."

Apostle Paul asked the disciples which he found in Ephesus, ***"Have ye received the Holy Ghost since ye believed?" (Acts 19:2)*** The scriptural references indicate that the Holy Ghost is a gift to all those who will meet the conditions. The conditions were stipulated by Apostle Peter on the day of Pentecost when he told the Jews in Jerusalem, ***"Repent and be baptized every one of you in the name of Jesus Christ for the remission of sins and ye shall receive the gift of the Holy Ghost. For the promise is unto you, and to your children, and to all that are afar off, even as many as the Lord our God shall call." (Acts 2:38-39)***

Christ, himself, proclaimed to his disciples after his resurrection that, ***"Ye shall receive power after that the Holy Ghost is come upon you." (Acts 1:8)*** In reference to the appearance of Christ in the flesh John declared, ***"He came unto his***

***own, and his own received him not. But as many as received him, to them gave he power to become the sons of God, even to them that believe on his name." (John 1:11-12)*** The Holy Ghost is a spiritual manifestation of the power of Almighty God given to the true believer as a gift. The recipient of this gift must first repent and secondly obey God's word. This is borne out in these Words of Peter: ***"And we are his witnesses of these things; and so is also the Holy Ghost, whom God hath given to them that obey him." (Acts 5:32)*** The gift of the power of the Holy Ghost cannot be received by oral declaration of acceptance. The Gift is described in the scriptures as a real dynamic manifestation of the power of God which is subject to the recipient as long as he or she is obedient to the Word of God.

Many denominations of Christianity erroneously ascribe little or no importance to the Holy Ghost as an active part in the lives of today's Christians. Some of them go so far as to teach the Holy Ghost was a gift of power for the early church only. There is no verification of this in any of the teachings of the Apostles. This concept would be contrary to Peter's declaration that ***"the promise is unto you, and your children, and to all that are afar off, even as many as the Lord our God shall call." (Acts 2:39)***

Some denominations teach the Holy Ghost is a spiritual frame of mind to be achieved by personal development of ones moral out-look. This teaching denies the dynamic power of the gift. Such a doctrine refuses to accept the charismatic influence on the life of a true Christian, as is so vividly demonstrated in lives of the early Christians recorded in the "Acts of the Apostles". Indeed, on the day of Pentecost the Charismatic influence on those recipients of this heavenly gift was so great they were under complete control of the spirit. They were heard to speak in languages which they themselves did not know. The biblical record states, ***"The spirit gave them utterance." (Acts 2:4)*** This type of demonstration occurred throughout the "Acts of the Apostles" whenever anyone became the recipient of the Holy Ghost.

The act of receiving the Holy Ghost is not recorded as a passive act as many would-be Christians believe. Instead, the reception of the heavenly gift was accompanied by such a demonstration of power that three thousand souls were added to the church in one day.

Peter and John went to the city of Samaria to pray for those which had been baptized in the name of the Lord Jesus, that they might receive the Holy Ghost. ***"Then laid they their hands on them, and they received the Holy Ghost. And when Simon*** (the sorcerer) ***saw that through laying on of the apostles' hands the Holy Ghost was given, he offered them money, saying, 'Give me also this power, that on whomsoever I lay hands, he may receive the Holy Ghost,'" (Acts 8:17-19)*** Surely Simon who, "used sorcery and bewitched the people", did not desire the power to instill in others a passive gift which was accompanied by no dynamic demonstrations of power.

Throughout the account of the lives of the apostles, the Holy Ghost performed many miracles and healings through the lives of the recipients. The record shows the Holy Ghost is a heavenly gift endowed with the mighty power of God. The scriptures teach that all believers are partakers of this heavenly gift. Without the indwelling power of the Holy Ghost, one cannot truthfully affirm his belief in God the Father, Jesus Christ, and the Holy Ghost.

When Christ commissioned his apostles he decreed, ***"Go ye into all the world, and preach the gospel to every creature. He that believeth and is baptized shall be saved; but he that***

***believeth not shall be damned. And these signs shall follow them that believe; In my name shall they cast out devils; they shall speak with new tongues; They shall take up serpents; and if they drink any deadly thing, it shall not hurt them; they shall lay hands on the sick, and they shall recover." (Mark 16:15-18)***

Apostle Paul prophesied, giving a very vivid description of the church world in the last days as well as a warning to those who would accept this form of Christianity. He said, ***"This know also, that in the last days perilous times shall come. For men shall be lovers of their own selves, covetous, boasters, proud, blasphemers, disobedient to parents, unthankful, unholy, without natural affection, trucebreakers, false accusers, incontinent, fierce, despisers of those that are good, traitors, heady, highminded, lovers of pleasures more than lovers of God; having a form of godliness, but denying the power thereof: from such turn away. For this sort are they which creep into houses, and lead captive silly women laden with sins, led away with divers lusts, ever learning and never coming to the knowledge of the truth." (II Timothy 3:1-6)*** Even the most tolerant of observers must admit this is certainly the conditions witnessed throughout Christendom today. Christianity without the dynamic power of the Holy Ghost is apostasy in its most abominable state.

To believe in the Holy Ghost is to experience the indwelling Spirit of God controlling the actions and thoughts of ones life. To be an acceptable Christian in the Kingdom of God, requires total submission of our being to the guidance of the Holy Ghost. John put it this way, ***"The anointing*** (Holy Ghost) ***which ye have received of him abideth in you, and ye need not that any man***

***teach you: but as the same anointing teacheth you of all things, and is truth, and is no lie, even as it hath taught you, ye shall abide in him. And now little children, abide in him; that, when he shall appear, we may have confidence, and not be ashamed before him at his coming." (I John 2:27-28)***

Christ became the living example to all that would follow in his footsteps. Above all else he denied himself. He did not seek after the personal pleasures of this life. He lived his life to benefit others. He neither requested nor accepted any recognition or remuneration for his many acts of benevolence. He was a minister in the true sense of the word, a servant to all mankind.

Although he accomplished so much, he never accepted credit as a man. When, ***"one came and said unto him, 'Good Master, what good thing shall I do, that I may have eternal life?" (Matthew 19:16)*** Prior to answering his question Christ admonished him by these words, ***"Why callest thou me good? There is none good but one, that is God*** (spirit): ***but if thou will enter into life, keep the commandments." (Matthew 19:17)*** He amplified these words when he said, ***"Believest thou not that I am in the Father, and the Father in me? The words that I speak unto you I speak not of myself: But the Father that dwelleth in me, he doeth the works." (John 14:10)***

Peter showed his understanding of the composition of the Godhead and its completeness in the begotten son, with these words, ***"God anointed Jesus of Nazareth with the Holy Ghost and with power; who went about doing good, and healing all that were oppressed of the devil; for God was with him."*** (In the form of the Holy Ghost). ***(Acts 10:38)***

By Christ's own words he shows us there is no good in man himself. To do good, a Christian must have God with him in the form of the indwelling Holy Ghost. Then and then only can we go about doing good in a selfless miraculous way, following in the footsteps of Christ. Then and only then can a Christian be perfect as Christ commanded all to be in his sermon on the mount. Without the gift of the Holy Ghost a would-be Christian cannot, ***"present his body a living sacrifice, holy, acceptable unto God, which is his reasonable service." (Romans 12:1)***

Paul told the Romans, ***"Let every soul be subject unto the higher powers. For there is no power but of God: The powers that be are ordained of God. Whosoever therefore resisteth the power, resisteth the ordinance of God: and they that resist shall receive to themselves damnation." (Romans 13:1-2)*** The power of God is manifested in the Holy Ghost.

"Suffered under Pontius Pilate, was crucified, dead, and buried:"

As we have seen, the scriptures plainly declare that God, an omnipotent Spirit was manifest in the flesh of man. Scripturally, this occurred, when the word which was with God, and as God, was made flesh and dwelt among men in the natural physical body of the begotten Son. Thus God became the son of man. Being omnipotent God, and all power, this manifestation certainly cannot be classified as impossible. Christ said, ***"With God all things are possible." (Mark 10:27)*** A true believer cannot rationalize God's ways according to man's ways. Isaiah says, ***"For my thoughts are not your thoughts, neither are your ways my ways, saith the Lord. For as the heavens are higher than the earth, so are my ways higher than your ways, and my thoughts than your thoughts." (Isaiah 55:8-9)***

At this point, one might ask why was it necessary that God the Spirit take on the flesh of man. The key to this answer is prophetically presented by John in the "Revelation of Jesus Christ". ***"And I saw a strong angel proclaiming with a loud voice, who is worthy to open the book, and to loose the seals thereof? And no man in heaven, nor in earth, neither under the earth, is able to open the book, neither to look thereon." (Revelations 5:2-3)*** Disregarding opening of the book, for the present, consider the unworthiness of man to accomplish this deed.

Man in his creation is not complete without the Spirit of God dwelling within his mortal body to reconcile him to God, his spiritual father. From the beginning of creation until the death of the begotten Son on the cross, man had proven his inadequacy. The Psalmist declares, ***"Verily every man at his best state is altogether vanity." (Psalms 39:5)*** Apostle Paul put it this way, ***"For all have sinned, and come short of the glory of God; being justified freely by his grace through the redemption that is in Christ Jesus: Whom God hath set forth to be a propitiation through faith in his blood, to declare his righteousness for the remission of sins that are past, through the forbearance of God. To declare, I say his righteousness: that he might be just, and the justifier of him which believeth in Jesus." (Romans 3:23-26)*** Therefore man cannot be righteous without the Spirit of God. Again Isaiah declares, ***"But we are all as an unclean thing, and all our righteousnesses are as filthy rags; and we all do fade as a leaf; and our iniquities, like the wind, have taken us away." (Isaiah 64:6) He also said, "All we like sheep have gone astray; we have turned every one to his own way: and the Lord hath laid on him the iniquity of us all." (Isaiah 53:6)***

Because man in his flesh is incomplete and unrighteous without the righteousness of God, he is lost, without hope and without God in the world. Man without God is vainly seeking happiness, trying desperately to replace the emptiness he has. Regardless of all his physical achievements, his vast riches, and his materialistic future, man cannot be happy without God. The Psalmist says, ***"Happy is he that hath the God of Jacob for his help, whose hope is in the Lord his God: which made heaven, and earth, the sea, and all that therein is: which keepeth truth for ever." (Psalms 146:5-6)*** He also says, ***"Happy is that people, that is in such case: Yea, happy is that people, whose God is the Lord." (Psalms 144:15)***

God, the creator of man, gave man ample time and opportunity to prove his inadequacy without God. He promised man redemption from his futile plight. Man in his natural state of unbelief would have to be shown that he could live righteous. Since this is impossible without the help of God, God manifested himself in the form of man. The fleshly body of Jesus became the begotten son of God, while also being the son of man.

As a human being subject to the will of the Spirit of God which dwelt in him, he was able to set the example for us to follow in his steps and attain to righteousness. Apostle Peter said, ***"For even hereunto were ye called: because Christ also suffered for us leaving us an example, that ye should follow his steps: who did no sin, neither was guile found in his mouth: who when he was reviled, reviled not again; when he suffered, he threatened not; but committed himself to him that judgeth righteously: who his own self bare our sins in his own body on the tree, that we, being dead to sins, should live unto righteousness: By whose stripes ye were healed. For ye were as sheep going astray; but are now returned unto the Shepherd and Bishop of your souls." (I Peter 2:21-25)*** Paul said, ***"And all things are of God, who hath reconciled us to himself by Jesus Christ, and***

***hath given to us the ministry of reconciliation." (II Corinthians 5:18)***

God thus gave us a high priest when he sent ***"His own son in the likeness of sinful flesh, and for sin condemned sin in the flesh: that the righteousness of the law might be fulfilled in us who walk not after the flesh but after the Spirit." (Romans 8:3-4) "For we have not an high priest which cannot be touched with the feeling of our infirmities, but was in all points tempted like as we are yet without sin." (Hebrews 4:15) "Forasmuch then as the children are partakers of flesh and blood, he also himself likewise took part of the same; that through death he might destroy him that had the power of death, that is the devil; and deliver them who through fear of death were all their lifetime subject to bondage. For verily he took not on him the nature of angels; but he took on him the seed of Abraham. Wherefore in all things it behooved him to be made like unto his brethren, that he might be a merciful and faithful high priest in things pertaining to God, to make reconciliation for the sins of the people. For in that he himself hath suffered being tempted, he is able to succour*** (help) ***them that are tempted." (Hebrews 2:14-18)***

These scriptures leave no doubt that the begotten son was in all points a human being, in flesh and blood and the offspring of David. He lived his human life righteous and without sin. He accomplished this because, ***"God anointed Jesus of Nazareth with the Holy Ghost and with power: who went about doing good, and healing all that were oppressed of the devil; for God was with him." (Acts 10:38)***

He, therefore, became our high priest and ***"By one offering he hath perfected for ever them that are sanctified." (Hebrews***

***10:14)*** By his life of obedience to the Spirit Father which dwelt in him, he lived a sinless perfect life as a man. The writer to the Hebrews puts it this way, ***"Then said he, Lo, I come to do thy Will O God. He taketh away the first*** (covenant) ***that he may establish the second. By the which will we are sanctified through the offering of the body of Jesus Christ once for all. And every high priest standeth daily ministering and offering oftentimes the same sacrifices, which can never take away sins: But this man, after he had offered one sacrifice for sins for ever, sat down on the right hand of God." (Hebrews 10:9-12)*** Thus he ***"Hath prevailed to open the book, and to loose the seven seals thereof." (Revelations 5:2)*** John wrote, ***"Thou art worthy to take the book, and to open the seals thereof: for thou wast slain, and hast redeemed us to God by thy blood out of every kindred, and tongue, and people, and nation; and hast made us unto our God kings and priests: and we shall reign on the earth." (Revelations 5:9-10)***

By following the example of Jesus Christ, man is able to be reconciled to God the Father of all mankind. Only then does he find himself complete and happy as a man. Through obedience to the words and example of Christ, man finds himself sanctified and separated from the ways of the world. Man finds this condition only comes by total submission to the Spirit of God the Father, dwelling in him, in the form of the gift of the Holy Ghost. Without the charismatic influence of the Holy Ghost, man is ***"Without God and without hope in this world." (Ephesians 2:12)***

To make this supreme sacrifice so man could be partaker of the heavenly gift of eternal life, it was necessary for God the Spirit to take on himself the flesh of man, live a sinless life, be crucified, (sacrificed) dead and buried. Without this sacrifice of the blood of

Jesus, no man would be able to open the Book of Life. Thus, God's plan of Salvation was made complete. Eternal Life was made available to all who obey his word, which he proclaimed was the selfsame word of God.

Paul unveiled the mystery of Godliness to Timothy when he said, ***"God was manifest in the flesh, justified in the Spirit, seen of angels, preached unto the Gentiles, believed on in the world, received up into Glory." (I Timothy 3:16)*** John said, ***"Hereby perceive we the love of God, because he laid down his life for us: and we ought to lay down our lives for the brethren." (I John 3:16)*** He also stated, ***"For God so loved the world, that he gave his only begotten Son,*** (His own body) ***that whosoever believeth in him should not perish, but have everlasting life." (John 3:16)***

To fulfill his plan of salvation for mankind, it was necessary for him to suffer death to the flesh. Because of his unselfish love for all mankind, God was obliged to lay down his life in the flesh as a means to prove death was subject to his power. When Pilate admonished Christ saying, ***"Knowest thou not that I have power to crucify thee, and have power to release thee?" (John 19:10)*** Jesus answered, ***"Thou couldest have no power at all against me, except it were given thee from above: therefore he that delivered me unto thee hath the greater sin." (John 19:11)***

His purpose is confirmed in these words of Paul to Titus, ***"For the grace of God that bringeth salvation hath appeared to all men, teaching us that, denying ungodliness and worldly lusts, we should live soberly, righteously, and godly, in this present world; looking for that blessed hope and the glorious appearing of the Great God and our Saviour Jesus Christ; who gave himself for us, that he might redeem us from all iniquity,***

***and purify unto himself a peculiar people, zealous of good works." (Titus 2:11-14)***

He could thus prove to all that eternal life is a reality, and available to all men; to those that would live Godly in this present world. It was only accomplished through the precedent established by the life, death, and resurrection of God manifested in the flesh. Paul told the Galatians, ***"Grace be to you and peace from God the Father, and from our Lord Jesus Christ, who gave himself for our sins, that he might deliver us from this present evil world, according to the will of God and our Father: to whom be glory for ever and ever. Amen." (Galatians 1:3-5)***

We see therefore, God the omnipotent Spirit did not die but instead life departed from the flesh of the begotten son on the cross, completing the example set forth for man by him. He opened up for all, the way to eternal life. Man need only follow in the footsteps of Christ the begotten son, obeying the word of God, repenting of his sins (which is the desire to please his own flesh), being baptized in the name of the one Lord Jesus Christ (which is the name of the Father, the Son, and the Holy Ghost), receiving the indwelling Spirit of God (which is the gift of the Holy Ghost), being led by the spirit. Only then can one "present his body a living sacrifice, holy, acceptable unto God," partaking of eternal life.

After he set the example, Christ was able to say, ***"I am the way, the truth, and the life: no man cometh unto the Father but by me." (John 14:6)*** He was also the door to the Kingdom of God for he said, ***"I am the door: by me if any man enter in he shall be saved, and shall go in and out and find pasture. The thief cometh not, but for to steal, and to kill, and to destroy: I am come that they might have life, and that they might have it more abundantly." (John 10:9-10)***

"He descended into hell, the third day he rose again from the dead."

Of all the tenets of the Apostles' Creed, this portion is the most misleading. It has been the subject of much controversy down through the ages. Investigation has shown it is the hardest part for the proclaimer to believe. The reason for this is the conditioning of the minds in the latter centuries.

The modern day vision of hell is a figment of the imagination passed down by early writers such as Dante Alighieri, born in Florence, Italy, in May, 1265. His description of hell gained such prominence that it was adopted as a reality. Due to the superstitious and ignorant nature of the populace of that day, this version of hell was readily accepted. It was particularly acceptable to those with a paganistic background. As a result, the mention of hell today causes most people to imagine a big hole in the center of the earth with bodies squirming in the flames. They also picture Satan there with horns and a long tail, holding his pitchfork. This picture of hell did not emanate from the biblical record. Like many false doctrines and traditions passed down through the ages, the classical picture of hell is founded on paganistic superstitions as well as the imaginations of the natural mind.

At the time the "Apostles' Creed" was formulated, this reference of "hell" carried the accurate biblical connotation. A detailed study of the biblical use of the word hell, as well as pit and grave will reveal the true meaning of hell as used in the Creed. In the Bible, hell is translated from two different meanings in the Hebrew and the Greek.

One meaning implies merely the place of the dead, or the grave, sometimes referred to as the earth or the depths of the earth. The word "pit", is also used interchangeably with grave to denote the trench dug into the earth as a place of burial. The word translated in the Old Testament having this definition, is from the Hebrew word "Sheol". The New Testament translation with this meaning is from the Greek word "Hades". Whenever Sheol or Hades is used in the original transcript, there is no connotation of everlasting punishment or torment associated with its meaning.

However, in some cases the finality of corporal punishment is indicated. Often, this is presented as conclusive retribution in the natural sense, for wickedness, in this life. The Psalmist states it this way, ***"Let death seize upon them, and let them go down quick into hell: for wickedness is in their dwellings and among them." (Psalms 55:15)*** He also said, ***"The sorrows of death compassed me, and the pains of hell gat hold upon me: I found trouble and sorrow."(Psalms 116:3)*** Solomon, in his reference to the evil of a strange woman and her demise said, ***"Her feet go down to death; her steps take hold on hell." (Proverbs 5:5)*** Thus he assured her associates an untimely death and burial.

The resurrected Christ spoke of his victory over death and the grave in this wise, ***"I am he that liveth and was dead; and, behold I am alive for evermore, Amen; and have the keys of hell and of death." (Revelations 1:18)***

Speaking of the resurrection of all that died, John the "Revelator" wrote concerning their return to life, and their final judgment. He said, ***"And I saw the dead, small and great, stand before God: and the books were opened: and another book was opened, which is the book of life: and the dead were judged out of those things which were written in the books, according to their works. And the sea gave up the dead which were in it; and death and hell delivered up the dead which were in them: and they were judged every man according to their works." (Revelations 20:12)***

The above reference denotes the term death and hell as merely the place of the dead buried in the earth. This is the true connotation as applied originally to this tenet of the "Apostles' Creed". The statement only affirmed that the proclaimer accepts the recorded account that Christ did in fact die a physical death, was buried in a grave, and subsequently rose from the grave to live again.

The Psalmist prophetically declares the words of Christ when he writes, ***"Therefore my heart is glad, and my glory rejoiceth: my flesh also shall rest in hope. For thou wilt not leave my soul in hell; neither wilt thou suffer thine Holy One to see corruption." (Psalms 16:10)*** Peter speaking to the Jews on the day of Pentecost as recorded in the "Acts of the Apostles" reiterated these words when he said, ***"For David speaketh concerning him; I foresaw the Lord always before my face, for he is on my right hand, that I should not be moved: Therefore did my heart rejoice, and my tongue was glad; moreover also my flesh shall rest in hope: Because thou wilt not leave my soul in hell, neither wilt thou suffer thine Holy One to see corruption. Thou hast made known to me the ways of life; thou shalt make me full of joy with thy countenance." (Acts 2:25-28)***

Apostle Paul discounted the significance of Christ's death and burial and stressed the emphasis on his resurrection in this statement to the Ephesians. ***"Now that he ascended, what is it but that he also descended first into the lower parts of the earth? He that descended is the same also that ascended up far above all heavens that he might fill all things." (Ephesians 4:9-10)***

Paul was attempting to show here that the important thing

was, that Christ had resurrected to life again. He provided a way of escape for all mankind from the otherwise inevitable destruction and damnation. Man could now achieve eternal life, by following the exemplary life of the Begotten Son. Salvation for man was completed. The "Gospel of Salvation" was thus established.

Paul told the Corinthians, ***"Now if Christ be preached that he rose from the dead, how say some among you that there is no resurrection of the dead? But if there be no resurrection of the dead, then is Christ not risen: And if Christ be not risen, then is our preaching vain, and your faith is also vain. Yea and we are found false witnesses of God; because we have testified of God that he raised up Christ: whom he raised not up, if so be that the dead rise not. For if the dead rise not, then is not Christ raised: and if Christ be not raised, your faith is vain; ye are yet in your sins. Then they also which are fallen asleep in Christ are perished. If in this life only we have hope in Christ, we are of all men most miserable. But now is Christ risen from the dead, and become the firstfruits of them that slept." (I Corinthians 15:12-20)***

He thus establishes that all the hope of a believer is dependent on the acceptance of the resurrection of Christ. Without the resurrection, there is no salvation available to man in his inadequate sinful state. There is no hope of reconciliation with God. Redemption comes only through Christ. Paul told the Romans, ***"It is Christ that died, yea rather, that is risen again, who is even at the right hand of God, who also maketh intercession for us." (Romans 8:34)***

Paul also told the Colossians, referring to Christ, ***"Who hath delivered us from the power of darkness, and hath translated us into the kingdom of his dear Son: In whom we*** *have redemption through his blood, even the forgiveness of sins: Who is the image of the invisible God, the firstborn of every creature: For by him were all things created, that are in heaven and that are in earth, visible and invisible, whether they be thrones, or dominions or principalities, or powers: all things were created by him and for him: And he is before all things, and by him all things consist. And he is the head of the body, the church: who is the beginning, the firstborn from the dead; that in all things he might have the preeminence.*

*For it pleased the Father that in him should all fullness dwell; and having made peace through the blood of his cross, by him to reconcile all things unto himself; by him, I say, whether they be things in earth, or things in heaven. And you that were sometimes alienated and enemies in your mind by wicked works, yet now hath he reconciled in the body of his flesh through death, to present you holy, unblamable, and unreproveable in his sight: if ye continue in the faith grounded and settled, and be not moved away from the hope of the gospel, which ye have heard, and which was preached to every creature which is under heaven; whereof I Paul am made a minister." (Colossians 1:13-23)*

Paul assured all of hope in the Gospel of Salvation through the resurrection of all, When he told the Corinthians, *"For we know that if our earthly house of this tabernacle* (the natural body) *were dissolved, we have a building of God, an house not made with hands, eternal in the heavens. For in this we groan, earnestly desiring to be clothed upon with our house which is from heaven." (II Corinthians 5:1-2) "For the love of Christ constraineth us; because we thus judge, that if one died for all, then were all dead: And that he died for all, that they which*

***live should not henceforth live unto themselves, but unto him which died for them and rose again." (II Corinthians 5:14-15)***

The writer to the Hebrews assures us, ***"But Christ being come an high priest of good things to come, by a greater and more perfect tabernacle, not made with hands, that is to say, not of this building: Neither by the blood of goats and calves, but by his own blood he entered in once into the holy place, having obtained eternal redemption for us." (Hebrews 9:11-12)*** Thus, his victory over death became mankind's victory over death if he would partake of his heavenly gift. God the Father Almighty, creator of heaven and earth, could not suffer defeat, ***"For there is no power but of God." (Romans 13:1)*** Isaiah foretold of Christ's victory over death and hell in these words, ***"He shall not fail nor be discouraged, till he have set judgment in the earth: and the isles shall wait for his law." (Isaiah 42:4)***

Should man choose to share in this victory over death and hell by fulfilling the requirements for the gift of Eternal Life, he will be saved from the other place often referred to in the scriptures as hell. The second meaning of the word hell in the Bible depicts a place or state of damnation and everlasting punishment and torment for the ungodly. This is contrasted with the place or state of eternal life and happiness for the obedient believer. In the Old Testament, this hell is translated from the Hebrew word "Gehinnom". In the New Testament, it is translated from the Greek word "Gehenna". It is from this meaning of hell, that the interpretation was accurately associated with fire. Through indiscriminate mixture of these different meanings of hell came forth the mystical interpretation of hell as a big hole or bottomless pit of fire. As stated before, this is an imaginary interpretation, not based on scripture rightly divided and understood. The final end is proclaimed by John in the book of

Revelations as follows: ***"He that overcometh shall inherit all things; and I will be his God, and he shall be my son. But the fearful, and unbelieving, and abominable, and murderers, and whoremongers, and sorcerers, and idolaters, and all liars, shall have their part in the lake which burneth with fire and brimstone: which is the second death." (Revelations 21:7-8)***

Because God, manifested in flesh, laid down his human life, descended into the grave and rose from the dead the third day the righteous believer can be delivered from this second death. He is promised eternal life if he will repent and live according to the Word of God.

Now that a way of Salvation was established and a door was opened to all through the life, death, burial and resurrection of the begotten son, man could be complete through the example of Christ. Paul told the Colossians, ***"Beware lest any man spoil you through philosophy and vain deceit, after the tradition of men, after the rudiments of the world and not after Christ. For in him dwelleth the fullness of the Godhead bodily. And ye are complete in him, which is the head of all principality and power: in whom also ye are circumcised with the circumcision made without hands, in putting off the body of the sins of the flesh by the circumcision of Christ: Buried with him in baptism, wherein also ye are risen with him through the faith of the operation of God, who hath raised him from the dead." (Colossians 2:8-12)***

# THE GODHEAD IN PERSPECTIVE

*"Beware lest any man spoil you through philosophy and vain deceit, after the tradition of men, after the rudiments of the world, and not after Christ. For in him dwelleth all the fulness of the Godhead bodily."*

*(Colossians 2:8-9)*

## GOD'S OMNIPOTENCE

*"Unto thee it was shown that thou mightest know that the Lord he is God; there is none else beside him.*

*Out of heaven he made thee to hear his voice, that he might instruct thee: and upon earth he showed thee his great fire; and thou heardest his words out of the midst of the fire.*

*And because he loved thy fathers, therefore he chose their seed after them, and brought thee out in his sight with his mighty power out of Egypt; to drive out the Nations from before thee greater and mightier than thou art, to bring thee in, to give thee their land for an inheritance, as it is this day.*

*Know therefore this day, and consider it in thine heart, that the Lord he is God in heaven above, and upon the earth beneath: there is none else." (Deuteronomy 4:35-39)*

*"Hear, O Israel: The Lord our God is one Lord: and thou shalt love the Lord thy God with all thine heart, and with all thy soul, and with all thy might." (Deuteronomy 6:4-5)*

*"See now that I, even I, am he, there is no God with me: I kill, and I make alive; I wound, and I heal: neither is there any that can deliver out of my hand." (Deuteronomy 32:39)*

*"Wherefore thou art great, O Lord God: for there is none like thee, neither is there any God beside thee, according to all that we have heard with our ears." (II Samuel 7:22)*

*"Ye are my witnesses, saith the Lord, and my servant whom I have chosen; that ye may know and believe me, and understand that I am he: before me there was no God formed, neither shall there be after me. I even I am the Lord; and beside me there is no saviour." (Isaiah 43:10-11)*

*"Thus saith the Lord the King of Israel, and his redeemer the Lord of Hosts; I am the first, and I am the last; and beside me there is no God. And who as I, shall call and shall declare it, and set it in order for me, since I appointed the ancient people? and the things that are coming, and shall come, let them shew unto them.*

*"Fear ye not, neither be afraid: have not I told thee from that time, and have declared it? Ye are even my witnesses. Is there a God beside me? yea, there is no God; I know not any." (Isaiah 44:6-8)*

*"For thus saith the Lord that created the heavens; God himself that formed the earth and made it; he hath established it, he created it not in vain, he formed it to be inhabited: I am the Lord; there is none else.*

*I have not spoken in secret, in a dark place of the earth: I said not unto the children of Jacob, Seek ye me in vain: I the Lord speak righteousness, I declare things that are right.*

*Assemble yourselves and come; draw near together, ye that are escaped of the nations: they have no knowledge that set up the wood of their graven image, and pray unto a God that cannot save.*

*Tell ye, and bring them near together: who hath declared*

*this from ancient time? who hath told it from that time? have not I the Lord? and there is no God else beside me; a just God and a Saviour; there is none beside me. Look unto me, and be ye saved, all the ends of the earth: for I am God, and there is none else." (Isaiah 45:18-22)*

## THE BEGOTTEN SON IN PERSPECTIVE

*"Now the birth of Jesus Christ was on this wise: When as his mother Mary was espoused to Joseph, before they came together, she was found with child of the Holy Ghost.*

*Then Joseph her husband, being a just man, and not willing to make her a public example, was minded to put her away privily.*

*But while he thought on these things, behold, the angel of the Lord appeared unto him in a dream, saying, Joseph, thou son of David, fear not to take unto thee Mary thy wife: for that which is conceived in her is of the Holy Ghost.*

*And she shall bring forth a son, and thou shall call his name JESUS: for he shall save his people from their sins.*

*Now all this was done, that it might be fulfilled which was spoken of the Lord by the prophet, saying, Behold, a virgin shall be with child, and shall bring forth a son, and they shall call his name Emmanuel, which being interpreted is, God with us." (Matthew 1:18-23)*

It is established that the begotten son was a human child and not a Deity or God; howbeit that he was conceived by the manifesting power of God, (the Holy Ghost) and God was his only natural father. The begotten son did not become ***"God with us"*** until his baptism in the river Jordan by John the Baptist, when the Holy Ghost descended and dwelt in him. ***(Matthew 3:13-17)***

This is further attested to by the writer of the Acts of the Apostles, where he states: ***"That word, I say, ye know, which was published throughout all Judea, and began from Galilee, after the Baptism which John preached; How God anointed Jesus of Nazareth with the Holy Ghost and with power: who went about doing good, and healing all that were oppressed of the devil; for God was with him." (Acts 10:37-38)***

The begotten son was Jesus of Bethlehem at birth. He did not become Jesus of Nazareth until some time after his return from Egypt and before his baptism by John. At that time, he was anointed with the Holy Ghost and with power.

The begotten son, Jesus Christ himself declared, ***"God is a Spirit: and they that worship him must worship him in spirit and in truth. (John 4:24)***

***"And all things are of God, who hath reconciled us to himself by Jesus Christ, and hath given to us the ministry of reconciliation.***

***To wit, God was in Christ, reconciling the world unto himself, not imputing their trespasses unto them; and committed unto us the word of reconciliation." (II Corinthians 5:18-19)***

With God in the form of the indwelling Holy Ghost in him, after his baptism by John, he was able to say. ***"I and my Father are one." (John 10:30)*** He never declared himself in flesh alone as deity.

Once God was in him or with him in the form of the Holy Ghost he was able to do many mighty works, or rather the Father which was in him did the works.

Jesus, the begotten son, explained it to Philip this way: ***"Jesus saith unto him, Have I been so long time with you, and*** *yet hast thou not known me, Philip? he that hath seen me hath seen the Father; and how sayest thou then, Shew us the Father?*

*Believest thou not that I am in the Father, and the Father in me? the words that I speak unto you I speak not of myself: but the Father that dwelleth in me, he doeth the works.*

*Believe me that I am in the Father, and the Father in me:* (in the form of the Holy Ghost) *or else believe me for the very works sake." (John 14:9-11)*

Apostle Paul put it this way: *"Beware lest any man spoil you through philosophy and vain deceit, after the tradition of men, after the rudiments of this world, and not after Christ. For in him dwelleth all the fullness of the Godhead bodily." (Colossians 2:8-9) "Let this mind be in you which was in Christ Jesus: Who, being in the form of God, thought it not robbery to be equal with God: But made himself of no reputation, and took upon him the form of a servant, and was made in the likeness of men: and being found in fashion as a man, he humbled himself, and became obedient unto death, even the death of the cross.*

*Wherefore God also hath highly exalted him, and given him a name which is above every name: That at the name of Jesus every knee should bow, of things in heaven, and things in the earth, and things under the earth; and that every tongue should confess that Jesus Christ is Lord, to the glory of God the Father.*

*Wherefore, my beloved, as ye have always obeyed, not as in my presence only, but now much more in my absence, work out your own salvation with fear and trembling." (Philippians 2:5-12)*

*"God, who at sundry times and in divers manners spake in time past unto the fathers by the prophets, hath in these last days spoken unto us by his Son, whom he hath appointed heir of all things, by whom also he made the worlds; who being the brightness of his glory, and the express image of his person, and upholding all things by the word of his power, when he had by himself purged our sins, sat down on the right hand of the majesty on high; being made so much better than the angels, as he hath by inheritance obtained a more excellent name than they.*

*For unto which of the angels said he at any time, Thou art my Son, this day have I begotten thee? And again, I will be to him a Father, and he shall be to me a son? And again, when he bringeth the first begotten into the world, saith, And let all the angels of God worship him. And of the angels he saith, who maketh his angels spirits, and his ministers a flame of fire.*

*But unto the Son he saith, Thy throne, O God, is for ever and ever: a sceptre of righteousness is the sceptre of thy kingdom.*

*Thou hast loved righteousness, and hated iniquity; therefore God, even thy God, hath anointed thee with the oil of gladness above thy fellows.*

*And thou, Lord, in the beginning hast laid the foundation of the earth; and the heavens are the works of thine hands: They shall perish; but thou remainest; and they all shall wax old as doth a garment; And as a vesture shalt thou fold them up, and they shall be changed: but thou art the same, and thy years shall not fail.*

*But to which of the angels said he at any time, Sit on*

*my right hand, until I make thine enemies thy footstool? Are they not all ministering spirits, sent forth to minister for them who shall be heirs of salvation?*

*Therefore we ought to give the more earnest heed to the things which we have heard, lest at any time we should let them slip. For if the word spoken by angels was stedfast, and every transgression and disobedience received a just recompense of reward; How shall we escape, if we neglect so great a salvation; which at first began to be spoken by the Lord, and was confirmed to us by them that heard him; God also bearing them witness, both with signs and wonders, and divers miracles, and gifts of the Holy Ghost, according to his own will?*

*For unto the angels hath he not put in subjection the world to come, whereof we speak. But one in a certain place testified, saying, What is man, that thou art mindful of him? or the son of man, that thou visitest him?*

*Thou madest him a little lower than the angels; thou crownest him with glory and honour, and didst set him over the works of thy hands: Thou hast put all things in subjection under his feet. For in that he put all in subjection under him, he left nothing that is not put under him. But now we see not yet all things put under him.*

*But we see Jesus, who was made a little lower than the angels for the suffering of death, crowned with glory and honour; that he by the grace of God shall taste death for every man.*

*For it became him, for whom are all things, and by whom are all things, in bringing many sons unto glory, to make the captain of their salvation perfect through sufferings.*

*For both he that sanctifieth and they who are sanctified are all of one: for which cause he is not ashamed to call them brethren, saying, I will declare thy name to my brethren, in the midst of the church will I sing praise unto thee.*

*And again, I will put my trust in him. And again, I and the children which God hath given me.*

*Forasmuch then as the children are partakers of flesh and blood, he also himself likewise took part of the same; that through death he might destroy him that had power of death, that is, the devil; and deliver them who through fear of death were all their lifetime subject to bondage.*

*For verily he took not on him the nature of angels; but he took on him the seed of Abraham. Wherefore in all things it behooved him to be made like unto his brethren, that he might be a merciful and faithful high priest in things pertaining to God, to make reconciliation for the sins of the people. For in that he himself hath suffered being tempted, he is able to succour them that are tempted.*

*Wherefore, holy brethren, partakers of the heavenly calling, consider the Apostle and High Priest of our profession, Christ Jesus; who was faithful to him that appointed him, as also Moses was faithful in all his house.*

*For this man was counted worthy of more glory than Moses, inasmuch as he who hath builded the house hath more honour than the house. For every house is builded by some man; but he that built all things is God.*

*And Moses verily was faithful in all his house, as a servant, for a testimony of those things which were to be spoken after; But Christ as a son over his own house; whose house are we, if we hold fast the confidence and the rejoicing of the hope firm unto the end.*

*Wherefore (as the Holy Ghost saith, To day if ye will hear his voice, harden not your hearts, as in the provocation, in the day of temptation in the wilderness: when your fathers tempted me, proved me, and saw my works forty years.*

*Wherefore I was grieved with that generation, and said, They do always err in their heart; and they have not known my ways. So I sware in my wrath, They shall not enter into my rest).*

*Take heed, brethren, lest there be in any of you an evil heart of unbelief, in departing from the living God. But exhort one another daily, while it is called to day; lest any of you be hardened through the deceitfulness of sin.*

*For we are made partakers of Christ, if we hold the beginning of our confidence stedfast unto the end; while it is said, to day if ye will hear his voice, harden not your hearts, as in the provocation. For some, when they had heard, did provide: howbeit not all that came out of Egypt by Moses.*

*But with whom was he grieved forty years? was it not them that had sinned, whose carcasses fell in the wilderness? And to whom sware he that they should not enter into his rest, but to them that believed not? So we see that they could not enter in because of unbelief.*

*Let us therefore fear, lest, a promise being left us of entering into his rest, any of you should seem to come short of it. For unto us was the gospel preached, as well as unto them: but the word preached did not profit them, not being mixed with faith in them that heard it.*

*For we which have believed do enter into rest, as he said, As I have sworn in my wrath, if they shall enter into my rest: although the works were finished from the foundation of the world.*

*For he spake in a certain place of the seventh day on this wise, And God did rest the seventh day from all his works. And in this place again, if they shall enter into my rest.*

*Seeing therefore it remaineth that some must enter therein, and they to whom it was first preached entered not in because of unbelief: Again, he limiteth a certain day, saying in David, To day, after so long a time; as it is said, To day if ye will hear his voice, harden not your hearts. For if Jesus had given them rest, then would he not afterward have spoken of another day.*

*There remaineth therefore a rest to the people of God. For he that is entered into his rest, he also hath ceased from his own works, as God did from his.*

*Let us labour therefore to enter that rest, lest any man fall after the same example of unbelief.*

*For the word of God is quick, and powerful, and sharper than any two-edged sword, piercing even to the dividing asunder of soul and spirit, and of the joints of marrow, and is a discerner of the thoughts and intents of the heart.*

*Neither is there any creature that is not manifest in his sight: but all things are naked and opened unto the eyes of him with whom we have to do.*

*Seeing then that we have a great high priest, that is passed into the heavens, Jesus the Son of God, let us hold fast our profession.*

*For we have not a high priest which cannot be touched with the feeling of our infirmities; but was in all points tempted like as we are, yet without sin. Let us therefore come boldly unto the throne of grace, that we may obtain mercy, and find grace in time of need.*

*For every high priest taken from among men is ordained for men in things pertaining to God, that he may offer both gifts and sacrifices for sins: who can have compassion on the ignorant, and on them that are out of the way; for that he himself also is compassed with infirmity. And by reason hereof he ought, as for the people, so also for himself, to offer for sins. And no man taketh this honour unto himself, but he that is called of God, as was Aaron.*

*So also Christ glorified not himself to be made an high priest; but he that said unto him, Thou art my Son, to day have I begotten thee. As he saith also in another place, Thou art a priest for ever after the order of Melchisedec.*

*Who in the days of his flesh, when he had offered up prayers and supplications with strong crying and tears unto him that was able to save him from death, and was heard that he feared; Though he were a Son, yet learned he obedience by the things which he suffered; and being made perfect, he became the author of eternal salvation unto all them that obey him; called of God an high priest after the order of Melchisedec.*

*Of whom we have many things to say, and hard to be uttered, seeing ye are dull of hearing. For when for the time ye ought to be teachers, ye have need that one teach you again which be the first principals of the oracles of God; and are become such as have need of milk, and not of strong meat. For every one that useth milk is unskillful in the word of righteousness: for he is a babe.*

*But strong meat belongeth to them that are of full age, even those who by reason of use have their senses exercised to discern both good and evil.*

*Therefore having the principles of the doctrine of Christ, let us go on unto perfection; not laying again the foundation of repentance from dead works, and of faith toward God, of the doctrine of baptisms and of laying on of hands, and of resurrection of the dead, and of eternal judgment.*

*And this will we do if God permit. For it is impossible for those who were once enlightened, and have tasted of the heavenly gift, and were made partakers of the Holy Ghost. And have tasted of the good word of God, and the powers of the world to come, if they shall fall away, to renew them again unto repentance; seeing they crucify to themselves the Son of God afresh, and put him to an open shame.*

*For the earth which drinketh in the rain that cometh oft upon it, and bringeth forth herbs meet for them by whom it is dressed, receiveth blessing from God: but that which beareth thorns and briars is rejected, and is nigh unto cursing; whose end is to be burned.*

*But beloved, we are persuaded better things of you, and things that accompany salvation, though we thus speak. For God is not unrighteous to forget your work and labour of love, which ye have shewed toward his name, in that ye have ministered unto the saints, and do minister.*

*And we desire that every one of you do shew the same diligence to the full assurance of hope unto the end: that ye be not slothful, but followers of them who through faith and patience inherit the promises.*

*For when God made promise to Abraham, because he could swear by no greater, he sware by himself. Saying, surely blessing I will bless thee, and multiplying I will multiply*

***thee.***

***And so, after he had patiently endured, he obtained the promise.***

***For men verily swear by the greater: and an oath for confirmation is to them an end of all strife. Wherein God, willing more abundantly to shew unto the heirs of promise the immutability of his counsel, confirmed it by an oath: that by two immutable things, in which it was impossible for God to lie, we might have a strong consolation, who have fled for the refuge to lay hold upon the hope set before us. Which hope we have as an anchor of the soul, both sure and stedfast, and which entereth into that within the veil; whither the forerunner is for us entered, even Jesus, made an high priest for ever after the order of Melchisedec." (Hebrews 1:1-6:20)***

Jesus Christ, the begotten Son was a natural human being, an offspring of Abraham and David, the natural son of Mary, and his conception was a result of supernatural power without a natural human father. Howbeit, as the begotten Son of God he was created to fulfill a divine commission. That commission being, to show man the way to eternal salvation by example.

In his natural human state, he did not have the power to fulfill his commission, thus because of his obedience and willingness to carry out his commitment. ***"God anointed Jesus of Nazareth with the Holy Ghost and with power: who went about doing good, and healing all that were oppressed of the devil; for God was with him." (Acts 10:38)*** Thus, he became a priest, for ever after the order of Melchisedec.

The Gospel of Jesus Christ, (the good news) was that if his fellow man would follow his example of life in submission to God and obedience to his own calling, each could receive the same Holy

Ghost with power, to become a true son of God, with eternal salvation. For God would be with them and in them. ***"For as many as are led by the Spirit of God, they are the sons of God." (Romans 8:14)***

## THE HOLY GHOST IN PERSPECTIVE

The omnipotent, omniscient, omnipresent, almighty God, manifests himself through the power of his Spirit: sometimes referred to as the Spirit of God, the Holy Spirit, the Holy Ghost, the Spirit of Christ, the Spirit of truth, the Comforter, or the Indwelling Spirit. These titles all refer to the active power of God.

Throughout the Bible, God manifested his power through others. ie: his Angels (messengers), or specially chosen individuals. They were usually chosen because of their ardent trust, belief in, and obedience to God. Since Christ showed us the way in his example, all men have available this opportunity.

The begotten Son, Jesus Christ, being one of those so chosen, as God was his supernatural Father, through the manifestation of God's power in the Holy Ghost, was made a human example for us to follow.

***"For even hereunto were ye called: because Christ also suffered for us, leaving us an example, that ye should follow in his steps: who did no sin, neither was guile found in his mouth: who when he was reviled, reviled not again; when he suffered, he threatened not: but committed himself to him that judgeth righteously: who his own self bare our own sins in his own body on the tree, that we, being dead to sins, should live unto righteousness: by whose stripes ye were healed. For ye were as sheep going astray; but are now returned to the shepherd and bishop of your souls." (I Peter 2:21-25)***

*"Then cometh Jesus from Galilee to Jordan unto John, to be baptized of him. But John forbad him saying, I have need to be baptized of thee, and comest thou to me?*

*And Jesus answering said unto him, Suffer it to be so now: for it becometh us to fulfil all righteousness. Then he suffered him.*

*And Jesus, when he was baptized, went up straightway out of the water: and, lo, the heavens were opened unto him, and he saw the Spirit of God descending like a dove, and lighting upon him: and lo a voice from heaven saying, This is my beloved Son, in whom I am well pleased." (Matthew 3:13-17)*

*"Believe thou not that I am in the Father, and the Father is in me? The words that I speak unto you I speak not of myself: but the Father that dwelleth in me, he doeth the works.*

*Believest me that I am in the Father, and the Father in me: or else believe me for the very works' sake.*

*Verily, verily, I say unto you, He that believeth on me, the works that I do shall he do also; and greater works than these shall he do; because I go unto the Father. And whatsoever ye shall ask in my name, that will I do, that the Father may be glorified in the Son.*

*If ye shall ask anything in my name, I will do it. If ye love me, keep my commandments. And I will pray the Father, and he shall give you another comforter, that he may abide in you for ever; even the Spirit of truth; whom the world cannot receive, because it seeth him not, neither knoweth him: but ye know him; for he dwelleth with you, and shall be in you.*

*I will not leave you comfortless: I will come to you.*

*Yet a little while, and the world seeth me no more; but ye see me: because I live, ye shall live also. At that day ye shall know that I am in my Father, and ye in me, and I in you.*

*He that hath my commandments, and keepeth them, he it is that loveth me: and he that loveth me shall be loved of my Father, and I will love him, and will manifest myself to him.*

*Judas saith unto him, not Iscariot, Lord, how is it that thou wilt manifest thyself unto us, and not unto the world? Jesus answered and said unto him, If a man love me he will keep my words: and my Father will love him, and we will come unto him, and make our abode with him.*

*He that loveth me not keepeth not my sayings: and the word which ye hear is not mine, but the Father's which sent me. These things have I spoken unto you, being yet present with you.*

*But the Comforter, which is the Holy Ghost, whom the Father will send in my name, he shall teach you all things, and bring all things to your remembrance, whatsoever I have said unto you.*

*Peace I leave with you, my peace I give unto you: not as the world giveth, give I unto you. Let not your heart be troubled, neither let it be afraid." (John 14:10-27)*

*"Until the day in which he was taken up, after that he through the Holy Ghost had given commandments unto the apostles whom he had chosen: To whom also he shewed himself alive after his passion by many infallible proofs, being seen of them forty days, and speaking of things pertaining to the kingdom of God: And, being assembled together with them, commanded them that they should not depart from Jerusalem, but wait for the promise of the Father, which, saith he, ye have*

*heard of me.*

*For John truly baptized with water; but ye shall be baptized with the Holy Ghost not many days hence.*

*When they therefore were come together, they asked of him, saying, Lord, wilt thou at this time restore again the kingdom of Israel?*

*And he said unto them, It is not for you to know the times and the seasons, which the Father hath put in his own power. But ye shall receive power, after that the Holy Ghost is come upon you: and ye shall be witnesses unto me both in Jerusalem, and in all Judea, and in Samaria, and the uttermost part of the earth." (Acts 1:2-8)*

*"And when the day of Pentecost was fully come, they were all with one accord in one place. And suddenly there came a sound from heaven as of a rushing mighty wind, and it filled all the house where they were sitting. And there appeared unto them cloven tongues like as of fire, and it sat upon each of them.*

*And they were all filled with the Holy Ghost, and began to speak with other tongues, as the Spirit gave them utterance." (Acts 2:1-4)*

*"Then Peter said unto them, Repent, and be baptized every one of you in the name of Jesus Christ for the remission of sins, and ye shall receive the gift of the Holy Ghost. For the promise is unto you, and to your children, and to all that are afar off, even as many as the Lord our God shall call." (Acts 2:38-39)*

God is Spirit. God is one. The Holy Ghost is the manifesting Power of God. Jesus Christ was God's begotten son, in flesh and blood, and God was in him in the form of the Holy

Ghost. Therefore, God was in him and with him.

*"And all things are of God, who hath reconciled us to himself by Jesus Christ, and hath given to us the ministry of reconciliation; to wit, God was in Christ, reconciling the world unto himself, not imputing their trespasses unto them; and hath committed unto us the word of reconciliation.*

*Now then we are the ambassadors for Christ, as though God did beseech you by us: we pray you in Christ's stead, be ye reconciled to God." (II Corinthians 5:18-20)*

*"Beware lest any man spoil you through philosophy and vain deceit, after the tradition of men, after the rudiments of the world, and not after Christ. For in him dwelleth all the fullness of the Godhead bodily." (Colossians 2:8-9)*

# GOD'S PLAN OF SALVATION ACCORDING TO THE BIBLE

*"For even hereunto were ye called: because Christ also suffered for us, leaving us an example, that ye should follow his steps: who did no sin, neither was guile found in his mouth: who when he was reviled, reviled not again; when he suffered, he threatened not: but committed himself to him that judgeth righteously: Who his own self bare our own sins in his own body on the tree, that we, being dead to sins, should live unto righteousness: by whose stripes ye were healed. For ye were as sheep going astray; but are now returned unto the Shepherd and Bishop of your souls."*

*I Peter 2:21-25*

Apostle Peter, as an Apostle of Jesus Christ, in the above admonishment to us, warns us that we are commissioned to live our lives in the example of Christ and walk in his steps. He warns us that we should be dead to sins and live unto righteousness.

The word "Christian" is defined as, "one having the qualities demonstrated and taught by Jesus Christ". To be a "Christian" is to be a follower or "disciple" of Jesus Christ and his teachings. These teachings come to us directly from the words he spoke or indirectly through his "called" Apostles.

*"Then said Jesus unto his disciples. If any man will come after me, let him deny himself, and take up his cross and follow me." (Matthew 16:24)* He also said, *"I am the door: by me if any man enter in, he shall be saved, and shall go in and out, and find pasture." (John 10:9)*

To be saved is, "to receive salvation". Salvation is the act of saving us or preserving us for the gift of "eternal life" which will be received at the revelation of Jesus Christ, provided we obey his word and walk in his steps, or follow him. If we walk in his steps and live our lives the way he did as an example, we will be saved through Christ, (Through his example).

Jesus said, ***"Verily, verily, I say unto you, He that entereth not by the door into the sheepfold, but climbeth up some other way, the same is a thief and a robber. But he that entereth in by the door is the shepherd of the sheep. To him the porter openeth: and the sheep hear his voice:*** (the Word)***and he calleth his own sheep by name, and leadeth them out. And when he putteth forth his own sheep, he goeth before them, and the sheep follow him:*** (in his steps)***for they know his voice.*** (the Word) ***And a stranger they will not follow, but will flee from him: for they know not the voice of strangers". (John 10:1-5)*** The writer of John records, ***"And the word was made flesh, and dwelt among us, (and we beheld his glory, the glory of the only begotten of the father,) full of grace and truth." (John 1:14)***

Jesus put it another way, when he said, ***"I am the way, the truth, and the life: no man cometh unto the father, but by me*** (through his example).***" (John 14:6)***

***"Then Jesus said unto them, 'Verily, Verily, I say unto you, Moses gave you not that bread from heaven; but my Father giveth you the true bread from heaven. For the bread of God is he which cometh down from heaven, and giveth life unto the world.'"***

***"Then said they unto him, 'Lord evermore give us this bread'***

***And Jesus said unto them, I am the bread of life: he***

*that cometh to me shall never hunger; and he that believeth on me shall never thirst." (John 6:32-35)*

*"Verily, verily, I say unto you, he that believeth on me hath everlasting life. I am that bread of life. Your fathers did eat manna in the wilderness and are dead. This is the bread that cometh down from heaven, that a man may eat thereof, and not die. I am the living bread which came down from heaven: if any man eat of this bread, he shall live forever: and the bread that I will give is my flesh, which I will give for the life of the world." (John 6:47-51)*

*"In the beginning was the Word, and the Word was with God, and the Word was God. The same was in the beginning with God. ["God is a spirit", (John 4:24)] All things were made by him: and without him was not any thing made that was made. In him was life; and the life was the light* [enlightenment] *of men. And the light* [enlightenment] *shineth in darkness; and the darkness comprehended it not. There was a man sent from God, whose name was John. The same came for a witness, to bear witness of the light,* [Jesus Christ (see verses 10-18)] *that all men through him* [through his example of life] *might believe.*

*He* [John] *was not that light, but was sent to bear witness of that light. That was the true light, which lighteth every man that cometh into the world.*

*He was in the world, and the world was made by him, and the world knew him not. But as many as received him, to them gave he the power* [Holy Ghost] *to become the sons of God, even to them that believe on his name: which were born, not of blood, nor of the will of man, but of God.*

*And the Word was made flesh, and dwelt among us, [and*

*we beheld his glory, the glory as of the only begotten of the father.] full of grace and truth.*

*John bare witness of him and cried, saying, This was he of whom I spake, He that cometh after me is preferred before me: for he was before me. And of his fullness have all we received, and grace for grace. For the law was given by Moses, but grace and truth came by Jesus Christ.*

*No man hath seen God at any time;* [God is a spirit] *the only begotten Son, which is in the bosom of the Father, he hath declared him. (John 1:1-18)*

Jesus said, *"No man can come to me, except the Father which hath sent me draw him: and I will raise him up at the last day.*

*It is written in the prophets, and they shall all be taught of God. Every man therefore that hath heard, and hath learned of the Father, cometh unto me. Not that any man hath seen the Father, save he which is of God, he hath seen the Father.*

*Verily, verily, I say unto you, He that believeth on me hath everlasting life.*

*Your fathers did eat manna in the wilderness and are dead. This is the bread which cometh down from heaven, that a man may eat thereof, and not die. I am the living bread which came down from heaven: if any man eat of this bread, he shall live forever: and the bread that I will give is my flesh, which I will give for the life of the world.* (And the Word was made flesh and dwelt among us.)

*The Jews therefore strove among themselves, saying, How can this man give us his flesh to eat? (Answer: "the words that I speak unto you, they are spirit, and they are life." (John 6:63))*

*Then Jesus said unto them, Verily, verily, I say unto you, Except ye eat the flesh of the Son of man, and drink his blood, ye have no life in you. Whoso eateth my flesh, and drinketh my blood, hath eternal life; and I will raise him up at the last day.*

*For my flesh is meat indeed, and my blood is drink indeed. He that eateth my flesh, and drinketh my blood, dwelleth in me and I in him. As the living Father hath sent me, and I live by the Father: so he that eateth me, even he shall live by me.* (following in the steps of Christ as he follows his Father)

*This is that bread which came down from heaven: not as your fathers did eat manna, and are dead: he that eateth of this bread shall live for ever." (John 6:44-58)*

He said, *"Verily, Verily, I say unto you, He that heareth my word, and believeth on him that sent me, hath everlasting life, and shall not come into condemnation; but is passed from death unto life." (John 5:24)*

Jesus said, *"It is the spirit that quickeneth; the flesh profiteth nothing: the words that I speak unto you, they are spirit, and they are life." (John 6:63)*

James elaborated on this when he said, *"Wherefore lay apart all filthiness and superfluity of naughtiness, and receive with meekness the engrafted word, which is able to save your souls.*

*But be ye doers of the word, and not hearers only, deceiving your own selves. For if any man be a hearer of the word, and not a doer, he is like unto a man beholding his natural face in a glass: For he beholdeth himself, and goeth his way, and straightway forgetteth what manner of man he was.*

***But whoso looketh into the perfect law of liberty, and continueth therein, he being not a forgetful hearer, but a doer of the work, this man shall be blessed in his deed." (James 1:21-25)***

Jesus said, ***"Let not your heart be troubled: ye believe in God, believe also in me.***

***In my Father's house are many mansions:*** (abodes) ***if it were not so I would have told you. I go to prepare a place for you. And if I go and prepare a place for you, I will come again, and receive you unto myself: and where I am, there ye may be also. And whither I go ye know, and the way ye know.***

***Thomas saith unto him, Lord we know not wither thou goest; and how can we know the way?***

***Jesus saith unto him, I am the way, the truth, and the life: no man cometh to the Father, but by me.*** (by his example)

***If ye had known me, ye should have known my Father also: and from henceforth ye know him, and have seen him.***

***Philip saith unto him, Lord, shew us the Father, and it sufficeth us.***

***Jesus saith unto him, Have I been so long with you, and yet hast thou not known me, Philip? he that hath seen me hath seen the Father; and how saith thou then, shew us the Father? Believest thou not that I am in the Father, and the Father in me? the words that I speak unto you I speak not of myself: but the Father that dwelleth in me, he doeth the works.***

***Believe me that I am in the Father, and the Father in me: or else believe me for the very works sake.***

***Verily, verily, I say unto you, He that believeth on me, the works that I do shall he do also; and greater works than these shall he do: because I go unto my Father.***

*And whatsoever ye ask in my name, that will I do, that the Father will be glorified in the Son. If ye shall ask anything in my name, I will do it.*

*If ye love me, keep my commandments.*

*And I will pray unto the Father, and he will give you another comforter,* (Holy Ghost) *that he may abide with you for ever; Even the Spirit of Truth; whom the world cannot receive, because it seeth him not, neither knoweth him: but ye know him; for he dwelleth with you,* (in the form of Christ, the begotten son) *and shall be in you.* (in the form of the Holy Ghost) *I will not leave you comfortless: I will come to you.*

*Yet a little while, and the world seeth me no more; but ye see me: because I live, ye shall live also. At that day ye shall know that I am in my Father, and ye in me, and I in you.*

*He that hath my commandments, and keepeth them, he it is that loveth me: and he that loveth me shall be loved of my Father, and I will love him, and will manifest myself to him.*

*Judas said unto him, not Iscariot, Lord how is it that thou will manifest thyself unto us, and not unto the world? Jesus answered and said unto him, if a man love me he will keep my words: and my Father will love him, and we will come unto him, and make our abode with him.* (in the form of the indwelling Holy Ghost see verse 26)

*He that loveth me not keepeth not my sayings: and the word which ye hear is not mine, but the Father's which sent me.*

*These things have I spoken unto you, being yet present with you. But the Comforter, which is the Holy Ghost, whom the Father will send in my name, he shall teach you all things, and bring all things to your remembrance, whatsoever I have*

***said unto you.***

***Peace I leave with you, my peace I give unto you: not as the world giveth, give I unto you. Let not your heart be troubled, neither let it be afraid." (John 14:1-27)***

The above compilation of New Testament Scriptures are the rightly divided word of truth on the subject of salvation of the followers of Christ. A detailed study will find the compilation completely in context.

Jesus continued to admonish us to follow him the way he followed the Father. That is why he said, ***"Be ye therefore perfect, even as your Father which is in heaven is perfect." (Matthew 5:48)***

This was not a meaningless commandment, but is consistent throughout the theme of the above compilation on salvation.

Apostle Paul considered the search for salvation to be a serious commitment when he wrote to the Philippians saying, ***"Wherefore, my beloved, as ye have always obeyed, not as in my presence only, but now much more in my absence, work out your own salvation with fear and trembling." (Philippians 2:12)***

Apostle Peter went one step further with this commandment, ***"Wherefore gird up the loins of your mind, be sober, and hope to the end for the grace that is to be brought unto you at the revelation of Jesus Christ; as obedient children, not fashioning yourselves according to the former lusts in your ignorance:***

***But as he which has called you is holy, so be ye holy in all manner of conversation*** (behavior); ***Because it is written, be ye holy; for I am holy.***

***And if ye call on the Father, who without respect of persons judgeth according to every man's work, pass the time of***

***your sojourning here in fear: forasmuch as ye know that ye were not redeemed with corruptible things, as silver and gold, from your vain conversation*** (behavior) ***received by tradition from your fathers; But with the precious blood*** (life) ***of Christ, as of a lamb without blemish and without spot: Who verily was foreordained before the foundation of the world, but was manifest in these last times for you, who by him do believe in God, that raised him up from the dead, and gave him glory; that your faith and hope might be in God.***

***Seeing ye have purified your souls in obeying the truth through the Spirit unto unfeigned love of the brethren, see that ye love one another with a pure heart fervently: Being born again, not of corruptible seed, but of incorruptible, by the word of God, which liveth and abideth for ever.***

***For all flesh is as grass, and all the glory of man as the flower of grass. The grass withereth, and the flower thereof falleth away: But the Word of the Lord endureth for ever. And this is the Word which by the gospel is preached unto you." (I Peter 1:13-25)***

Seeing it is a serious matter to follow in the steps of Christ to perfection and holiness, a true follower of Christ cannot take this commitment lightly.

However, as Peter stated above: ***"all flesh is as grass and all the glory of man as the flower of grass".*** Man alone does not contain the power of self control to maintain his own behavior. The writer of John said, ***"He was in the world, and the world knew him not. He came unto his own, and his own received him not. But as many as received him, to them gave he power to become the sons of God, even to them that believed on his name: which were born, not of the blood, nor of the will of the flesh,***

***nor of the will of man, but of God." (John 1:10-13)***

Therefore, since man in himself does not have the inherent power to become Holy or perfect ***("as your Father which is in heaven is perfect")***, we as men must look to Christ, as our example, who was a man in flesh as we are, to determine what was the source of his power to be able to live perfect as he did, for our example.

***"Then cometh Jesus from Galilee to Jordan unto John to be baptized of him. But John forbad him saying, I have need to be baptized of thee, and comest thou to me?***

***And Jesus answering said unto him, Suffer it to be so now: for thus it becometh us to fulfil all righteousness. Then he suffered him.***

***And Jesus, when he was baptized, went up straightway out of the water: and lo, the heavens were opened unto him, and he saw the Spirit of God (the Holy Ghost) descending like a dove, and lighting upon him: and lo a voice from heaven, saying, This is my beloved Son in whom I am well pleased." (Matthew 3:13-17)***

Thus, the example was established by Jesus for all who would follow him.

The writer of the Acts of The Apostles recorded Peter's account this way: ***"Then Peter opened his mouth, and said, Of a truth I perceive that God is no respecter of persons: But in every nation he that feareth him, and worketh righteousness, is accepted with him.***

***The word which God sent unto the children of Israel, preaching peace by Jesus Christ: (he is Lord of all:) That Word I say, ye know, which was published throughout Judea, and began from Galilee, after the baptism of John was preached;***

*How God anointed Jesus of Nazareth with the Holy Ghost and with power: who went about doing good, and healing all that were oppressed of the devil; for God was with him." (Acts 10:34-38)*

Prior to Jesus being baptized of John in the river Jordan and being anointed by the Father (God), there is no record of Jesus doing any healings or miracles because he had not yet received the power which was endued from on high in the form of the indwelling Holy Ghost. (see Luke 24:49)

Jesus Christ's last words to his followers were, *"wait for the promise of the Father, which, ye have heard of me. (see John 14:16-27 and Luke 24:44-49.) For John truly baptized with water; ye shall be baptized with the Holy Ghost not many days hence."*

*When they therefore were come together, they asked of him, saying, Lord, wilt thou at this time restore again the kingdom of Israel?*

*And he said unto them, "It is not for you to know the times or the seasons, which the Father hath put in his own power. But ye shall receive power, after that the Holy Ghost is come upon you: and ye shall be witnesses* (examples) *unto me both in Jerusalem, and in Samaria, and unto the uttermost parts of the earth." (Acts 1:4-8)*

*"And when the day of Pentecost was fully come, they were all with one accord in one place. And suddenly there came a sound from heaven as of a rushing mighty wind, and it filled all the house where they were sitting. And there appeared unto them cloven tongues like as of fire, and it sat upon each of them.*

*And they were all filled with the Holy Ghost, and began*

*to speak with other tongues, as the Spirit gave them utterance." (Acts 2:1-4)*

They were, thus, following the example which Jesus Christ had set for them before, which was recorded by Matthew.

Apostle Paul recorded it this way. *"For the love of Christ constraineth us; because we thus judge, that if one died for all, then were all dead: and that he died for all, that they which live should not henceforth live unto themselves, but unto him which died for them, and rose again.*

*Wherefore henceforth know we no man after the flesh: yea though we have known Christ after the flesh, yet now henceforth know we him no more.*

*Therefore if any man be in Christ, he is a new creature: old things are passed away; behold, all things are become new. And all things are of God, who hath reconciled us to himself by Jesus Christ,* (by his example) *and hath given to us the ministry of reconciliation; To wit, that God was in Christ, reconciling the world unto himself, not imputing their trespasses unto them; and hath committed unto us the word of reconciliation.*

*Now we are ambassadors* (examples) *for Christ, as though God did beseech you by us: we pray you in Christ stead, be ye reconciled to God. (II Corinthians 5:14-20)*

When the disciples, following in the steps of Jesus Christ, received the power of the Holy Ghost, those who witnessed their subsequent behavior enquired of Peter, *"what shall we do"? "Then Peter said unto them, "Repent, and be baptized every one of you in the name of Jesus Christ for the remission of sins, and ye shall receive the gift of the Holy Ghost." (Acts 2:38)*

There is no record of any recession of this commandment to the present day. Rather Apostle Peter continued in the very next verse.

*"For the promise is unto you, and your children, and to all that are afar off, even as many as the Lord our God shall call. (Acts 2:39)*

Jesus established the necessity for all his followers to be baptized in water and Spirit as he had been, when John related the story of Nicodemus.

*"There was a man of the Pharisees, named Nicodemus, a ruler of the Jews: The same came to Jesus by night, and said unto him, Rabbi, we know that thou art a teacher come from God: for no man can do these miracles that thou doest, except God be with him.*

*Jesus answered and said unto him, Verily, verily, I say unto thee, Except a man be born again, he cannot see the kingdom of God. Nicodemus saith unto him, How can a man be born when he is old? Can he enter the second time into his mother's womb, and be born?*

*Jesus answered, Verily, verily, I say unto thee, except a man be born of water and of Spirit, he cannot enter into the kingdom of God. That which is born of the flesh is flesh; and that which is born of the Spirit is spirit. Marvel not that I said unto thee, Ye must be born again.*

*The wind bloweth where it listeth, and thou hearest the sound thereof, but canst not tell whence it cometh, and whither it goeth: so is every one that is born of the Spirit.*

*Nicodemus answered and said unto him, How can these things be? Jesus answered and said unto him, Art thou a master of Israel, and knowest not these things?*

*Verily, verily, I say unto thee, We speak that we do know, and testify that we have seen; and ye receive not our witness.*

*If I have told you earthly things, and ye believe not, how shall ye believe, if I tell you of heavenly things? And no man hath ascended up to heaven, but he that came down from heaven, even the Son of man which is in heaven. And as Moses lifted up the serpent in the wilderness, even so must the Son of man be lifted up: That whosoever believeth in him should not perish, but have eternal life.*

*For God so loved the world, that he gave his only begotten Son, that whosoever believeth in him should not perish, but have everlasting life.*

*For God sent not his Son into the world to condemn the world; but that the world through him might be saved* (through his example).

*He that believeth on him is not condemned: but he that believeth not is condemned already. because he has not believed in the name of the only begotten Son of God. And this is the condemnation, that light is come into the world, and men loved darkness rather than light, because their deeds were evil.*

*For every one that doeth evil hateth the light, neither cometh to the light, lest his deeds should be reproved. But he that doeth truth cometh to the light, that his deeds may be made manifest, that they are wrought in God. (John 3:1-21)*

*"There is therefore now no condemnation to them which are in Christ Jesus, who walk not after the flesh, but after the Spirit.*

*For the law of the Spirit of life in Christ Jesus hath made me free from the law of sin and death.*

*For what the law could not do, in that it was weak through the flesh, God sending his own Son in the likeness of sinful flesh, and for sin, condemned sin in the flesh: that the righteousness of the law might be fulfilled in us, who walk not after the flesh, but after the Spirit.*

*For they that are after the flesh do mind the things of the flesh; but they that are after the Spirit the things of the Spirit.*

*For to be carnally minded is death, but to be spiritually minded is life and peace.*

*Because the carnal mind is enmity against God: for it is not subject to the law of God, neither indeed can be. So then they that are in the flesh cannot please God.*

*But ye are not in the flesh, but in the Spirit, if so be that the Spirit of God dwell in you. Now if any man have not the Spirit of Christ, he is none of his. And if Christ be in you, the body is dead because of sin; but the Spirit is life because of righteousness.*

*But if the Spirit of him that raised up Jesus from the dead dwell in you, he that raised up Christ from the dead shall also quicken your mortal bodies by his Spirit that dwelleth in you.*

*Therefore, brethren, we are debtors, not to the flesh, to live after the flesh. For if ye live after the flesh, ye shall die: but if ye through the Spirit do mortify the deeds of the body, ye shall live.*

*For as many as are led by the spirit of God, they are the sons of God.*

*For ye have not received the spirit of bondage again to fear; but ye have received the Spirit of adoption, whereby we cry, Abba, Father. (Romans 8:1-15)*

*"Be ye not unequally yoked together with unbelievers:*

*for what fellowship hath righteousness with unrighteousness? and what communion hath light with darkness? And what concord hath Christ with Belial? or what part hath he that believeth with an infidel?*

*And what agreement hath the temple of God with idols? for ye are the temple of the living God; as God hath said, I will dwell in them, and walk in them; and I will be their God, and they shall be my people.*

*Wherefore come out from among them, and be ye separate, saith the Lord, and touch not the unclean thing; and I will receive you. And will be a Father to you, and ye shall be my sons and daughters, saith the Lord Almighty." (II Corinthians 6:14-18)*

*"Having therefore these promises, dearly beloved, let us cleanse ourselves from all filthiness of the flesh and spirit, perfecting holiness in the fear of God. (II Corinthians 7:1)*

*"Wherefore laying aside all malice, and all guile, and hypocrisies, and envies, and all evil speakings, as newborn babes, desire the sincere milk of the word, that ye may grow thereby: if so be that ye have tasted that the Lord is gracious.*

*To whom coming, as unto a living stone, disallowed indeed of men, but chosen of God, and precious, ye also, as lively stones, are built up a spiritual house, an holy priesthood, to offer up spiritual sacrifices, acceptable to God by Jesus Christ.*

*Wherefore also it is contained in the scriptures, Behold, I lay in Sion a chief corner stone, elect, precious: and he that believeth on him shall not be confounded.*

*Unto you therefore which believe, he is precious: but unto them which be disobedient, the stone which the builders disallowed, the same is made the head of the corner. And a stone of stumbling, and a rock of offence, even to them which stumble at the Word, being disobedient: whereunto also they were appointed.*

*But ye are a chosen generation, a royal priesthood, an holy nation, a peculiar people; that ye should show forth the praises to him who hath called you out of darkness into his marvelous light: which in times past were not a people, but are now the people of God: which had not obtained mercy, but now have obtained mercy.*

*Dearly beloved, I beseech you as strangers and pilgrims, abstain from fleshly lusts, which war against the soul; having your conversation* (behavior) *honest among the Gentiles: that, whereas they speak against you as evildoers, they may by your good works, which they shall behold, glorify God in the day of visitation.*

*Submit yourselves to every ordinance of man for the Lord's sake: whether it be to the king, as supreme; or unto governor's, as unto them that are sent by him for the punishment of evildoers, and for the praise of them that do well. For so is the will of God, that with well doing ye may put to silence the ignorance of foolish men: as free, and not using your liberty for a cloak of maliciousness, but as the servants of God.*

*Honour all men. Love the brotherhood. Fear God. Honour the king.*

*Servants, be subject to your masters with all fear; not only to the good and gentle, but also to the froward. For this is thankworthy, if a man for conscience toward God endure grief, suffering wrongfully.*

*For what glory is it, if when ye are buffeted for your faults, ye shall take it patiently? but if, when ye do well, and suffer for it, ye take it patiently, this is acceptable with God.*

*"For even hereunto were ye called: because Christ also suffered for us, leaving us an example, that ye should follow his steps: who did no sin, neither was guile found in his mouth: who when he was reviled, reviled not again; when he suffered, he threatened not: but committed himself to him that judgeth righteously: Who his own self bare our own sins in his own body on the tree, that we, being dead to sins, should live unto righteousness: by whose stripes ye were healed. For ye were as sheep going astray; but are now*
*returned unto the Shepherd and Bishop of your souls." (I Peter 2:1-25)*

## THE GREATEST HOAX

***"Beware lest any man spoil you through philosophy and vain deceit, after the traditions of men, after the rudiments of this world, and not after Christ. For in him dwelleth all the fulness of the Godhead bodily".***

***Colossians 2:8-9***

After the recordings of the scriptures, the New Testament Church continued to grow; and with that growth apostasy continued to flourish as carnal minds increased their influence. As a result many schisms emerged, each proclaiming to be the true basis for Christianity. However, there has always been a devout following of Christ's teachings and those of his personally selected Apostles.

Those professing the teachings of Christ and his Apostles found themselves continually engaged as the recipients of religious persecutions. After all Apostle Paul said, ***"But thou hast fully known my doctrine, manner of life, purpose, faith, longsuffering, charity, patience, persecutions, afflictions, which came unto me at Antioch, at Iconium, at Lystra; what persecutions I endured: but out of them all the Lord delivered me. Yea, and all that will live Godly shall suffer persecution". (II Timothy 3:10-12)***

History tells us that throughout the second and third century the persecutions against the true Christians continued; but could not extinguish the continued growth and influence of the teachings of Christ and his Apostles. Many true Christians were martyred for their convictions. This only caused them to continue their growth.

Finally, in the early fourth century, Eusebius, Bishop of Rome in the Pagan Church, came up with what he considered a clever scheme to obscure the true Christian. He managed to convince the new emperor Constantine to endorse Christianity as the state religion. This would put Christianity under the control of the Emperor himself. Since the true Christian was humble in nature and did not seek self recognition or reputation, the emperor would establish his own version of Christianity, and stem the tide of true Christianity. The unpretentious true Christian would pale in comparison to the highly acclaimed and acceptable new version of Christianity.

The true Christianity would continue to exist as always but would fade into obscurity without the continued publicity of religious persecutions. The true Christian continued to be persecuted; but without the public fanfare. The influence of the true Christian could thus be controlled.

Since the Emperor declared himself God and required his subjects to worship him alone as supreme being, it was not hard to pull this off, the greatest hoax ever perpetrated against mankind. At Eusebius coaxing the Emperor Constantine would fashion the new version of Christianity as close as possible to the generally acceptable paganistic religion and practices of the masses.

Eusebius referred to the Christian scriptures to formulate the tenets of this new religion to relate to the tenets already practiced in their form of paganism. The new religion had to have its "Queen of Heaven" or the "Queen Mother" to replace Semiramis: thus Mary the mother of Jesus was selected to fill this roll. Mary was elevated to the status of deity and was referred to as the "Mother of God".

Baby Jesus was selected to replace "Nimrod or Tamuz" the Son of the Queen of Heaven, himself proclaimed God in Pagan lore.

The unwitting pagan, being uneducated, ignorant and under the total subjection of the Emperor "God" did not know the difference.

The acceptance of the baby Jesus God, God almighty the Father, and The Holy Ghost, fulfilled the requirements of a religion which was "Polytheistic" in nature. Thus, the ignorant pagan was inducted into the new state religion without much objection. After all, who could object to the Emperor "God" himself.

To validate this new state religion, Eusebius conjured up the "Vision of Constantine". In this vision, Constantine is purported to have seen a vision appear to him in the sky. The vision was to have been a cross and the words, "with this cross, go forth and conquer". By acceptance of this vision, Constantine was to convert to Christianity, thereby instituting Christianity as the new State religion. Thus, Constantine publicly converted to Eusebius' version of the new Christianity. This new version of Christianity, was an acceptable mixture of "True Christianity and the practices of Paganism (Syncretism).

Eusebius even went so far as to provide identification for these converts to this false religion now called Christianity. He instituted the symbol of the fish as the identifying mark to distinguish the false Christians following Constantine's version from others who proclaimed to be Christians.

Thus, he could uncover the true Christians which were diligently following the teachings of Christ and his Apostles. They would not produce the identifying symbol of the fish, therefore they were subject to prosecution and elimination as enemies of the state. This caused the false religion to flourish and true Christianity to diminish, thus solving the problem of the true Christians popularity and influence.

The selection of the symbol of the cross and the symbol of

the fish came directly from Paganism. To the ignorant of Paganistic practices, Eusebius would pacify by referring to the scriptures of Jesus instructing Peter to *"go to the sea, and cast an hook, and take up the fish that first cometh up; and when thou hast opened his mouth, thou shalt find a piece of money: that take, and give to them for me and thee." (Matthew 17:27)*

The truth is, the fish is regarded as the highest symbol of life in the Pagan religion. The reason for this is the fish is the most prolific of animals along with rabbits and eggs, (all Pagan religious symbols).

As for the cross as a symbol, Eusebius felt safe in referring to the words of Paul when he said, *"For Christ sent me not to baptize, but to preach the gospel: not with wisdom of words, lest the cross of Christ should be made of none effect. For the preaching of the cross is to them that perish foolishness; but unto us which are saved it is the power of God." (I Corinthians 1:17-18)*

The truth is, Paul in the above reference to the cross is not referring to the physical wooden cross which was ultimately responsible for Christ's death. Instead, by implication he was referring to the agony of the cross, or the atonement of Christ. It remains incredible that anyone proclaiming to worship Christ would give any homage or veneration to the symbol of the physical cross which caused Christ such agony in death.

The symbol of the wooden cross has always been highly revered in the religion of Paganism. It was worshipped thousands of years before Christ. Its shape represented the letter "T", the initial of Tamuz the Pagan Sun God. False Christianity has blindly followed the teachings and traditions of Paganism, even after the Word of God himself declared these customs as abominations. No true Christian would dare to practice these customs if they knew better. Unfortunately, the preeminence of false Christianity and the lack of diligent study of the teachings of Christ and his Apostles, have left the would be true Christian deceived by the greatest hoax of all time.

The very vision of Constantine became the motivation for this writer to launch a "search for truth". It was found incredulous to the writer that God would give anyone a vision which would advocate one to perform acts which would be so diametrically opposed to his own word.

Christ declared, ***"Ye have heard that it hath been said, Thou shalt love thy neighbor, and hate thine enemy. But I say unto you, Love your enemies, bless them that curse you, do good to them that hate you, and pray for them which despitefully use you, and persecute you; that ye may be the children of your Father which is in heaven: for he maketh his sun to rise on the evil and on the good, and sendeth rain on the just and on the unjust. For if ye love them which love you, what reward have ye? do not even the publicans the same? And if ye salute your brethren only, what do ye more than others? do not even the publicans so?***

***Be ye therefore perfect, even as your Father which is in heaven is perfect". (Matthew 5:43-48)***

In following Christ's teaching, Apostle Paul told the Romans, ***"bless them which persecute you: bless, and curse not. Rejoice with them that do rejoice, and weep with them that weep. Be of the same mind one toward another. Mind not high things, but condescend to men of low estate. be not wise in your own conceits.***

***Recompense to no man evil for evil. Provide things***

***honest in the sight of all men. If it be possible, as much as lieth in you, live peaceably with all men.***

***Dearly beloved, avenge not yourselves, but rather give place to wrath: for it is written, Vengeance is mine; I will repay, saith the Lord.***

***Therefore if thine enemy hunger, feed him; if he thirst, give him drink: for in so doing thou shalt heap coals of fire on his head.***

***Be not overcome of evil, but overcome evil with good. (Romans 12:14-21)***

This is the teaching of "True Christianity" as expounded by Christ and the Apostles. How then can one claim to be Christian and "go forth and conquer", killing and ravaging in the name of Christianity. Such practices are continuing to this day as a result of following in Constantine's example.

To complete his control over his new found state religion, Constantine called the "Council of Nicea" into session in Rome, Italy on June 19, through August 25, 325 AD. All existing church bishops of the Pagan religion were invited to attend. The Council of Nicea thus became the birth place of what is now called "Catholicism".

With the syncretism of the new form of Christianity in place, Constantine was now free to go forth and conquer those that opposed his rule without the bothersome pestilence of true Christianity.

The following is the documented evidence of the formulation of the false Christianity of Constantine beginning with the "Council of Nicea". Prior to this meeting history does not provide any documented evidence that this version of Christianity ever existed.

Below is an excerpt from "The Encyclopedia of Religion,

Copyright 1987, page 125", which attempts to establish the history of "Christian Councils". This document was heavily influenced by the false history of Christianity as presented by the Catholic Church. A close review of this excerpt will show the lack of authentic history of "Christian Councils" until 325 AD. The input representing council history prior to 325 AD is very sparse and is an attempt to falsify history and make Constantine's Catholicism retroactive to the time of the Apostles meeting recorded in The Acts of the Apostles, (Acts Chapter 15).

As noted in the article, "The first attempt to gather a body of bishops representing the whole Christian world was the council called by the emperor Constantine I at Nicea".

The real truth is recorded as follows: **"The era of church building in Rome may be said to begin with the reign of Constantine and the peace of the church. Before then Christian worship was conducted with various degrees of secrecy either in private houses or in the Catacombs (q.v.), according as the reigning emperor viewed the sect with tolerance or dislike. The type of church which in the beginning of the fourth century was adopted with certain modifications from the pagan basilica, though varying much in size, had little or no variety in its general form and arrangement." (Encyclopaedia Britannica, 1892, Ninth edition, Vol. XX, page 833)**

This statement from the Encyclopaedia Britannica, would provide evidence that no organized Catholic Church existed prior to the Nicene Council in 325 AD.

**Christian Councils.** Since the beginning of Christian history, designated leaders of Christian communities have from time to time gathered to make authoritative decisions on common teaching and practice. Such gatherings are usually called councils or synods (from the Greek sunodos, "a coming together"). Although these two terms are sometimes used synonymously, especially in Greek-Christian literature, synod normally designates the gathering of representatives from a local church or a single denomination, as distinct from council, which usually means a meeting at which representation is intended to be universal. Although only seven such meetings, all held in Greek cities in Asia Minor between the fourth and eighth centuries, are recognized by most Christian churches today as worldwide, or "ecumenical," councils (from the Greek oikoumené, "the inhabited world") and as classically authoritative in their articulation of Christian faith and church order, the conciliar pattern of decision making has remained a constant feature in the life of most churches. The Roman Catholic church, in fact, has traditionally regarded fourteen later councils, most of them Western gatherings held under papal auspices, as also ecumenical and normative. Christian councils have varied greatly in size, procedure, composition, and the way in which they have been convoked and ratified. The only criterion for determining their authority and importance is the practical norm of "reception": that a council's decisions are subsequently accepted by a church or a group of churches as valid and binding.

**Councils in the Early Church.** Precedents for early Christian conciliar practice lay in the Jewish Sanhedrin, or national council of priests and elders, which regulated the religious affairs, as well as some secular matters, of postexilic Israel until the destruction of Jerusalem in AD 70, and in the collegial bodies of priest and leading citizens that ruled most local cults in the Hellenistic and Roman world. [See Sanhedrin.] The first recorded gathering of Christian leaders to rule in a doctrinal and disciplinary dispute was the "council" of apostles and elders held in AD 48 or 49 and described in Acts of the Apostles 15:6-29. That council decided not to require full observance of the Mosaic law from gentile converts. As the Christian church established itself in other regions of the Greco-Roman world, special meetings of the bishops in a particular province or region were occasionally called to deal with disputed issues, such as the prophetic Montanist movement (Asia Minor, c. 170), the date of the celebration of Easter (Asia Minor, Palestine, Gaul, and Rome, c. 190), the readmission to Christian communion of those who had "lapsed" in persecution (Rome, c. 230-250; Carthage, c. 240-250), or the scandalous behavior of Paul of Samosata, bishop of Antioch (Antioch, 264-268).

During the late second and third centuries, episcopal synods probably met regularly in most regions, although the evidence is fragmentary. As the end of the illegal status of the Christian churches drew near, however, their leaders became bolder in organizing such meetings. A synod of Spanish bishops held in Elvira, near Granada, some time in the first decade of the fourth century enacted eighty-one canons on church discipline that remained widely influential, particularly on the indissolubility of marriage and clerical celibacy. Another local synod, as Aries in southern Gaul (August 314), called to consider the response of Catholics to the schismatic Donatist church in Africa, ruled against rebaptizing Donatists who wished to enter the Catholic church.

**Early Ecumenical Councils.** The first attempt to gather

a body of bishops representing the whole Christian world was the council called by the emperor Constantine I at Nicea, in northwest Asia Minor, in the summer of 325 (19 June-25 August). The Council of Nicea is still recognized as the first ecumenical Christian council and as the model for later authoritative gatherings. With the style and procedure of the Roman senate likely in mind, Constantine commissioned the 318 bishops who had assembled near his residence in Nicea, including several representatives from the Latin church of the West, to settle the controversy raised by Arius's denial of the eternity and full divinity of Jesus. In asserting that Jesus, as Son of God, is "begotten, not made" and "of the same substance as the Father" the council's creedal formula laid the groundwork for the classical development of Christian trinitarian theology in the half century that followed. [See Creeds, article on Christian Creeds.] The Nicene council also excommunicated Arius and his followers, determined a unified way of reckoning the date of Easter, and issued twenty disciplinary decrees or canons, mainly regulating the appointment and jurisdiction of bishops. Although the emperor's influence was strongly felt at Nicaea, it was the bishops themselves--under the leadership of Constantine's adviser, Bishop Hosius of Cordova, and of the young Alexandrian priest Athanasius--who formulated common theological and practical decisions. The bishops of the whole Christian world were now publicly recognized as the senate of the church.

After more than fifty years of sharp controversy over the reception and interpretation of the Nicene formula, a period that saw the proliferation of local synods and the production of many new creeds, the emperor Theodosius I convoked a meeting of some 150 Greek-speaking bishops at Constantinople in 381 (May-July) for council (Constantinople I). In addition to confirming Nicaea's insistence on the full divinity of Jesus as Son, this council condemned those who denied that the Holy Spirit is a distinct individual within the trinitarian mystery of God. An expanded version of the Nicene Creed, probably professed by the patriarch-elect Nectarius during the council before his installation in the see of Constantinople, was taken by the Council of Chalcedon (451) to be the official creed of the whole gathering and is still used as the standard profession of faith in many Christian liturgies (the "Niceno-Constantinopolitan Creed"). This council also enacted four disciplinary canons, including one that accord second place in ecclesiastical honor, after that of "old Rome", to the new imperial capital, Constantinople. That provision was to become a cause of contention between the Eastern and Western churches.

As a result of a bitter dispute between Nestorius, bishop of Constantinople, and Cyril, bishop of Alexandria, over the proper way of conceiving the relationship of the divine and human aspects of Jesus, the emperor Theodosius II summoned a meeting of bishops at Ephesus on the coast of Asia Minor, in the summer of 431, to resolve the issue, and more particularly to judge the propriety of calling Mary "Mother of God" (theotokos), as Cyril insisted on doing. Representatives of the opposing groups could not agree to meet, and the would-be council ended abortively in mutual excommunication. Later (April 433), Cyril came to an agreement with the more moderate of Nestorius's supporters to excommunicate Nestorius and to accept the title theotokos as valid, but also to recognize that in Jesus two distinct natures--the human and the divine--are united without confusion in a single individual. On the basis of this agreement, the meeting of Cyril's party at Ephesus in 431 later came to be regarded as the third ecumenical council, and the dossier assembled there by Cyril's supporters was used as a classical anthology of christological documents.

The fullest articulation of the early church's understanding of the person of Christ was made at a council held at Chalcedon, across the Bosporus from Constantinople, in the fall of 451 (October-November). In response to continuing controversy over whether the humanity of Jesus constituted a distinct and operative reality or "nature" after the incarnation of the Word, the emperor Marcian convoked this meeting of over 350 bishops (including three legates from Pope Leo I and two North African bishops) and forced it to formulate a doctrinal statement on Christ that accommodated a variety of theological traditions. The chief inspiration of the document, however, was the balanced "two-nature" Christology articulated by Leo in his letter to Bishop Flavian of Constantinople in 449. The council also enacted twenty-eight disciplinary canons, the last of which confirmed the second rank of the see of Constantinople and awarded it jurisdictional primacy in Asia Minor and northeastern Greece. This meeting, regarded as the fourth ecumenical council, as the first for which we possess detailed minutes as well as final documents.

Chalcedon's formulation of the Christian understanding of Christ proved to be only a new beginning for controversy. After more than a century of recriminations, especially in the East, the emperor Justinian I convoked another meeting at Constantinople (Constantinople II) in the year 553 (5 May-2 June) and persuaded the 168 bishops present to reformulate the

Christology of Chalcedon in terms that more clearly emphasized the centrality of Jesus' divine identity. They also condemned the speculative theology of Origen (third century) and his followers, as well as that of the chief opponents of Cyril of Alexandria from the previous century. The Roman bishop, Vigilius I, was present in Constantinople during the council but refused to attend, suspecting--along with most Western bishops--that it was being forced to weaken the stated faith of Chalcedon in the interests of political unity, In February 554, however, he agreed to accept the decisions of Constantinople II, a step that resulted in decades of controversy in Italy and Africa. This synod has generally been accepted since then as the fifth ecumenical council.

In the century that followed, Greek theologians continued to look for ways of reconciling the monophysites, Christians who had broken from the official church after Chalcedon by emphasizing the dynamic unity of the two-natured Christ as a divine person. One such attempt, favored by several seventh-century Byzantine patriarchs and emperors, was the ascription to Christ of a single divine will and "activity", or range of behavior. Led by the exiled Greek monk Maximos the Confessor, a local Roman synod of October 649 rejected this new Christology as a subtle weakening of the integral affirmation of Jesus' humanity. This condemnation was confirmed by a small gathering of mainly Eastern bishops in the rotunda of the imperial palace in Constantinople between 7 November 680 and 16 September 681, a synod subsequently recognized as the sixth ecumenical council (Constantinople III).

Ten years later, the emperor Justinian II summoned another gathering of bishops in the same rotunda to discuss disciplinary issues and formulate practical canons that would supplement the authoritative theological decisions of Constantinople II and III. Hence its customary titles, the "Quinisext" (fifth-and-sixth) synod or the synod "in the rotunda" (Gr., en trulló), also known as the Trullan synod. The membership of this meeting was also entirely Greek, and a number of its canons explicitly rejected Western practices. Although this gathering is not regarded as ecumenical, its legislation became one of the main sources of Orthodox canon law and was also frequently cited by Western medieval canonists.

The main theological controversy in the eighth- and ninth-century Eastern church was no longer directly over the person of Christ, but over the related issue of the legitimacy of using and venerating images in the context of worshiping a transcendent God. In 726, Emperor Leo III began the policy of removing and destroying the images in churches (iconoclasm), and his successor, Constantine V, convoked a synod of 338 bishops in Constantinople in 754 to ratify this practice, excommunicating those who defended the use of images, including the theologian and monk John of Damascus. [See Iconoclasm.] In 787 (24 September-7 October), however, the empress Irene convoked another synod at Nicaea (Nicaea II), attended by some 350 Greek bishops and two papal representatives. This synod reversed the decision of the year 754 and affirmed the legitimacy of venerating images and of asking for the intercession of the saints, while insisting also that worship, in the strict sense, is due to God alone. A resurgence of iconoclastic influence in the early ninth century delayed full acceptance of this council's decrees in the East, while the rivalry of the emperor Charlemagne and the poor Latin translation of the acts of Nicaea

II that reached his court led to resistance in the West and even to condemnation of the council's decisions at a synod of 350 bishops at Frankfurt in June 794. However, Nicaea II was recognized as the seventh ecumenical council at the Council of Constantinople (869-870), a recognition that was endorsed for the West by Pope John VIII in 880. It is the last of the ancient councils recognized as authoritative by virtually all Christian churches. (End of Excerpt).

As documented in the above excerpt, Constantine's false Christianity was ensnarled in confusion for over four centuries; and has not ceased to be in confusion to this day. Apostle Paul said, ***"For God is not the author of confusion, but of peace, as in all churches of the saints." (I Corinthians 14:33)*** If Paul was right, then Christ was not the author of Constantine's false Christianity. The truth of Christ's teachings has been readily available in the scriptures of the Holy Bible all along; and has not changed to this day.

A very crude though successful attempt to legitimize this "new Christianity" was completed at the "Council of Nicaea". This writer will delineate in the following pages many of the techniques, acts, concepts, and practices which were established and incorporated in the formulation of this "Christianity in wolves clothing".

The word Catholic by definition means, "universal". By declaration, Constantine thus decreed the new false version of Christianity as the universal world church, the only authentic Christianity. He further decreed that any not considering themselves Catholic could only be accepted as heretics. These heretics included the then true Christian which believed in following the teachings of Christ and his apostles and not the decrees of the Catholic Church.

This is the position of the Catholic Church until this day. With this self proclaimed universal authority, the Catholic church has found it completely within their authority to modify and actually change the teachings, customs, traditions, and practices of true Christianity, even though Christ taught the "Word of God", which he declared cannot be broken. The Psalmist said, ***"Forever O Lord, thy word is settled in heaven". (Psalms 119:89)*** Isaiah said, ***"The grass withereth, the flower fadeth: but the word of our God shall stand for ever." (Isaiah 40:8)***

Christ also said, ***"For verily I say unto you, Till heaven and earth pass, one jot or one tittle shall in no wise pass from the law, till all be fulfilled."(Matthew 5:18)***

In spite of these scriptures establishing the immutability of God's word, the Catholic Church feels free to change the viability of God's Word from time to time for the purposes which suit the existing regime of the period. The Catholic church somehow feels it has the authority to change Christianity at will. This they do in spite of the established written word.

The Catholic Church has made a concerted effort to modify church history through the years. A diligent "searcher for truth" can compare even the Catholic documents and see how time has changed the record.

An excellent example is to compare the changing record of the different Catholic Encyclopaedia editions over the years. This is not an easy task as many of the older editions have been destroyed. A careful search will uncover existing copies. The rewriting of church history by the Catholic Church is no less than astounding. This powerful influence has extended to secular documents as well, ie: secular encyclopaedias, dictionaries, and history books.

The 1905 edition of the Catholic Encyclopaedia openly

admits that there is no historical evidence that Apostle Peter ever went to Rome. The subsequent 1907 edition and later versions replaces this view with an explanation of suppositions that Peter indeed must have gone to Rome and was crucified there. This fraudulent effort was made to support the false premise that the Church of St. Peter in Rome was built on Peters grave, as well as give credence to the location of the Holy See in Rome. Just one of the many falsehoods used to deceive the aspiring Christian.

For the diligent "searcher for truth", there is a great preponderance of evidence available. There is available evidence to prove that even some of the letters of early church writers (prior to 325 AD) have been tampered with and forged paragraphs have been inserted to attempt to retroactively validate the existence of Catholicism to the time of Christ.

The most blatant of these falsehoods is the Catholic teaching that Christ declared Apostle Peter the first Pope of the Catholic Church. For the unlearned this premise could be accepted; but a close look of what Christ had to say will unquestionably eradicate such a premise. The truth severs the connection of Christ with the Catholic Church.

***"When Jesus came into the coasts of Caesarea Philippi, he asked his disciples, saying, Whom do men say that I the Son of man am? And they said, Some say that thou art John the Baptist: some, Elias; and others, Jeremias, or one of the prophets. He saith unto them, But whom say ye that I am? And Simon Peter answered and said, Thou art the Christ, the Son of the living God.***

***And Jesus answered and said unto him, Blessed art thou, Simon Barjona: for flesh and blood hath not revealed it unto thee, but my Father which is in heaven. And I say unto thee,***

*That thou art Peter, and upon this rock I will build my church; and the gates of hell shall not prevail against it. And I will give unto thee the keys of the kingdom of heaven: and whatsoever thou shalt bind on earth shall be bound in heaven: and whatsoever thou shalt loose on earth shall be loosed in heaven." (Matthew 16:13-19)*

Considering this passage alone it is easy to understand how the unlearned could accept this premise, that Christ was bestowing some special honor on Peter, but lets look at Peters conception of Christ's words when he said, "On this rock I will build my church".

*"And it came to pass on the morrow, that their rulers, and elders, and scribes, and Annas the high priest, and Caiaphas, and John, and Alexander, and as many as were of the kindred of the high priest, were gathered together at Jerusalem.*

*And when they had set them in the midst, they asked, By what power, or by what name have ye done this? Then Peter, filled with the Holy Ghost, said unto them, Ye rulers of the people, and elders of Israel, If we this day be examined of the good deed done to the impotent man, by what means he is made whole; Be it known unto you all, and to all the people of Israel, that by the name of Jesus Christ of Nazareth, whom ye crucified, whom God raised from the dead, even by him doth this man stand here before you whole.*

*This is the stone which was set at naught of you builders, which is become the head of the corner. Neither is there salvation in any other: for there is none other name under heaven given among men, whereby we must be saved". (Acts 4:5-12)*

Peter, thus, established to the rulers of Israel that he fully understood Christ's declaration, when Christ said, *"on this rock* (himself the cornerstone which was rejected of the builders of Israel) ***I will build my church, and the gates of hell*** (referring to the grave which he told them God raised him from the dead) ***shall not prevail against it"***. Peter well understood Christ was referring to himself and not to Peter as the first pope.

Further proof is found that all the Apostles understood Christ was the rock on which his church was built. Apostle Paul informed the Corinthians, ***"Moreover, brethren, I would not that ye should be ignorant, how that all our fathers were under the cloud, and all passed through the sea; and were all baptized unto Moses in the cloud and in the sea; and did all eat the same spiritual meat; and did all drink of the same spiritual drink: for they drank of that spiritual rock that followed them: and that rock was Christ. (I Corinthians 10:1-4)***

Apostle Paul told the Ephesians, ***"Now therefore ye are no more strangers and foreigners, but fellow citizens with the saints, and of the household of God; and are built upon the foundation of the apostles and prophets, Jesus Christ himself being the chief corner stone; in whom all the building fitly framed together groweth unto an holy temple in the Lord: In whom ye also are builded together for an habitation of God through the Spirit". (Ephesians 2:19-22)***

The premise of Peter being commissioned as the first pope is therefore totally baseless and is purposely intended to deceive and draw would be Christians away from the truth. Since the very foundation of the Catholic Church as genuine Christianity is based solely on this false premise, then it only stands to reason that the remaining claims to validity are suspect. If the foundation of Catholicism is obviously a false premise, the searcher for truth must look at church history circumspectly.

A cursory view of the "Cessation of Popes", if not so tragic would be no less than hilarious. It is very obvious to the learned that this document was prepared after 325 AD. Just take a look at the reference to Clement of Rome and compare this entry with the scriptural reference to Clement. You can easily see how weak the foundation was for this document, especially with the lack of historical evidence to support the existence of popes prior to the fourth century. The truth is that Constantine in fact was the first pope of the Catholic Church which he formulated in 325 AD. Any information to the contrary, no matter how voluminous, must be reviewed with the utmost detail, and suspicion.

Of all those proclaiming to be Christian followers of Christ and his apostles, the teachings of the Catholic church, when compared to the written word, fails miserably to the test of the teachings of Christ and his apostles. This is true even when the Catholic Duay/Confraternity version of the Holy Bible, with the imprimatur, is used for the comparison.

Let us cite a few examples of how the Catholic church chooses to ignore or reject the teachings of Christ and his apostles.

The ecclesiastical structure of the Catholic Church did not originate in the teachings of Christ and his Apostles, nor from the customs and traditions of the Holy Scriptures. The Levitical Priesthood of the Old Testament Judaism in no way resembles the structure of the Catholic Church.

The Catholic Church, being structured in a Pagan society was required to maintain a semblance of Polytheism while embracing the popular practices of idolatrous ritualistic worship. The false Christianity of Constantine was therefore patterned after the customs of the popular religion of the day while incorporating just enough of the scriptures to appear to emanate from the source of true Christianity. This new synchretism was then accepted by the populace. It did not matter what the true follower would believe, since every effort would be used to discredit any objection.

The ecclesiastical structure of the Catholic Church was therefore structured after Pagan worship and authority. There was expectation that any major opposition to the state religion would be quelled by the power and authority of the state government. This indeed was the case to the point where all opposition was curtailed to allow Constantine's Christianity to be accepted without too much interference, from true Christianity.

As mentioned above, the Council of Nicea established the doctrine of the Trinity. This doctrine incorporated a polytheistic God, which has no foundation in scripture. According to scripture God is a spirit, (Christ's own words) The begotten son was flesh and blood, the offspring of Abraham and David. The very foundation doctrine like that premise which made Peter the first pope is totally erroneous.

Unlike the teaching of the Catholic Church, Apostle Paul wrote to Timothy, ***"For there is one God, and one mediator between God and men, the man Christ Jesus; who gave himself a ransom for all, to be testified in due time". (I Timothy 2:5-6)*** The Catholic Church would have us to believe the contrary, that the Catholic priest is a mediator between God and men.

Even if Christ made Peter the Vicar of himself, his only commission to Peter was to "feed my sheep". Peter, himself, understood the authority of the ministry of Christ's Christianity. He wrote, ***"The elders which are among you I exhort, who am also an elder, and a witness of the sufferings of Christ, and also a partaker of the glory that shall be revealed: Feed the flock of God which is among you, taking the oversight thereof, not by*** *constraint, but willingly; not for filthy lucre, but of a ready mind; neither as being lords over God's heritage, but being examples to the flock. And when the chief Shepherd shall appear, ye shall receive a crown of glory that fadeth not away". (I Peter 5:1-4)* This is not commensurate with the position of authority and control exercised by the Catholic hierarchy.

Jesus Christ, himself, made clear that ecclesiastical hierarchy would have no place among his followers, therefore in his own words he denounced church structure which placed one man above another in authority and control.

Mark records it this way, *"But Jesus called them to him, and saith unto them, Ye know that they which are accounted to rule over the Gentiles exercise lordship over them; and their great ones exercise authority upon them. But so shall it not be among you: but whosoever will be great among you, shall be your minister (servant): And whosoever of you will be the chiefest, shall be servant of all. For even the Son of man came not to be ministered unto, but to minister, and to give his life a ransom for many. (Mark 10:42-45)*

The Catholic Church however, regardless of Christ's teaching, saw fit to follow the strong Pagan influence of its founders and instituted an ecclesiastical hierarchy diametrically opposed to the very humble aspects of true Christianity.

Unlike the practices of the Catholic hierarchy, Christ and his Apostles taught all leaders of God's people to lead by example not by control. Apostle Paul taught the Galatians, *"For brethren, ye have been called into liberty; only use not liberty for an occasion to the flesh, but by love serve one another. For all the law is fulfilled in one word, even in this; Thou shalt love thy neighbor as thyself. (Galatians 5:13-14)*

Jesus led by example at the last supper. ***"He riseth from supper, and laid aside his garments; and took a towel, and girded himself. After that he poureth water into a basin, and began to wash the disciples' feet, and to wipe them with the towel wherewith he was girded.***

***Then cometh he to Simon Peter: and Peter said unto him, Lord, dost thou wash my feet? Jesus answered and said unto him, What I do thou knowest not now; but thou shalt know hereafter.***

***Peter saith unto him, Thou shalt never wash my feet. Jesus answered him, If I wash thee not, thou hast no part with me. Simon Peter saith unto him, Lord, not my feet only, but also my hands and my head.***

***Jesus saith unto him, He that is washed needeth not save to wash his feet, but is clean every whit: and ye are clean, but not all. For he knew who would betray him; therefore said he, Ye are not all clean.***

***So after he had washed their feet, and had taken his garments, and was set down again, he said unto them, Know ye what I have done to you ? Ye call me Master and Lord: and ye say well; for so I am. If I then your Lord and Master, have washed your feet; ye also ought to wash one another's feet. For I have given you an example, that ye should do as I have done to you.***

***Verily, verily, I say unto you, The servant is not greater than his lord; neither he that is sent greater than he that sent him. If ye know these things, happy are ye if ye do them." (John 13:4-17)***

This example which Jesus so dramatically demonstrated to his disciples at the last supper proved he did not esteem one person greater than another. After all, he was the chiefest among them but that made him servant of all. (See Mark 10:42-45) Though he, being Lord and Master, and chiefest of them all, humbled himself to do homage to all. He thus taught his ministers were servants to his followers and were not greater in any respect to the followers of Christ. The word minister is defined: attendant, or servant.

How then could an ecclesiastical hierarchy structured in such a way that each person would be required to pay homage or veneration to those above him in rank, claim to be the ministry of Christ's Christianity. A simple comparison of Christ's relationship to his followers, and the pope of the Catholic Church's relationship to the Catholics will prove the Catholic Church is an obvious impostor and a fraud.

## THE END OF FALSE CHRISTIANITY

*"Let God arise, let his enemies be scattered: let them also that hate him flee before him".*

*Psalms 68:1*

Apostle John, in his recordings of "The Revelation of Jesus Christ, (sometimes referred to as The Apocalypse of John)", documents his heavenly vision, which records in prophetic form, the existence of the false Christianity to come.

He wrote, *"And I stood upon the sand of the sea, and saw a beast rise up out of the sea, having seven heads and ten horns, and upon his horns ten crowns, and upon his heads the name of blasphemy.*

*And the beast which I saw was like unto a leopard, and his feet were as the feet of a bear, and his mouth as the mouth of a lion: and the dragon gave him his power, and his seat, and great authority. And I saw one of his heads and as it were wounded to death; and his deadly wound was healed: and all the world wondered after the beast.*

*And they worshipped the dragon which gave power to the beast: and they worshipped the beast, saying who is like unto the beast? Who is able to make war with him?*

*And there was given unto him a mouth speaking great things and blasphemies; and power was given unto him to continue forty and two months. And he opened his mouth in blasphemy against God, to blaspheme his name, and his tabernacle, and them that dwell in heaven.*

*And it was given unto him to make war with the saints, and to overcome them: and power was given him over all kindreds, and tongues, and nations. And all that dwell upon the earth shall worship him, whose names are not written in the book of life of the lamb slain from the foundation of the world.*

*If any man have an ear, let him hear." (Revelations 13:1-9)*

Later in his documentation, John explains in more detail that the above reference is to that power which created Paganism with its blasphemies against God and his followers (saints). We would be led to believe that Paganism preexisted true Christianity. Christ's teachings were established "before the foundation of the world". Christ's teachings were those of true Judaism. He was condemned and crucified for denouncing those expounding false Judaism and Paganism.

John went on in prophecy and said, *"And I beheld another beast coming up out of the earth; and he had two horns like a lamb, and spake as a dragon. And he exerciseth all the power of the first beast before him, and causeth the earth and them which dwell therein to worship the first beast, whose deadly wound was healed.*

*And he doeth great wonders, so that he maketh fire come down from heaven on the earth in the sight of men, and deceiveth them that dwell on the earth by the means of those miracles which he had power to do in the sight of the beast; saying to them that dwell on the earth, that they should make an image to the beast, which had the wound by a sword, and did live.*

*And he had power to give life unto the image of the beast, that the image of the beast should both speak, and cause*

***that as many as would not worship the image of the beast should be killed.***

***And he causeth all, both small and great, rich and poor, free and bond, to receive a mark in their right hand, or in their foreheads: and that no man might buy or sell, save he that had the mark, or the name of the beast, or the number of his name.***

***Here is wisdom. Let him that hath understanding count the number of the beast: for it is the number of a man; and his number is Six hundred threescore and six." (Revelations 13:11-18)***

The revealing aspects of this prophecy is readily available to the searcher for truth to this day. A close inspection of the lettering on the mitre (headress) of the Roman Catholic Pope will spell out in Roman Numerals the number 666. This is a well known fact to the learned. Therefore, according to this prophecy, Constantine the head and founder of the Roman Catholic Church, is the second beast of Revelation chapter 13.

"He had the horns of a lamb; but spake like a dragon". He falsely represented the lamb (Christ) but carried out the wishes of the first beast of Revelation, chapter 13, which was and is the satanic power and evil influence of Paganism, Nimrod. He causes the earth and them that dwell therein to unwittingly worship the first beast, thinking all the time they are sincerely worshipping Christ. The Catholic Church is, according to this prophecy, a dangerous wolf in sheep's (lamb's) clothing.

The proof continues. The Miter, or headress of the pope, bishops, and abbots, when examined closely, came not from Judaism as some would have us believe, but came directly out of Paganism. The shape of the miter is that of the forward portion of a fish with mouth open. The fish is the foremost symbol of Paganism due to it's powers of fertility and reproduction. The doctrines and ritualistic worship of sex, fertility, and reproduction, is an abomination to God.

The prophecy of Revelation continues, *"And there followed another angel, saying Babylon is fallen, is fallen, that great city, because she made all nations drink of the wine of the wrath of her fornication.*

*And the third angel followed them, saying with a loud voice, If any man worship the beast and his image, and receive his mark in his forehead, or in his hand, the same shall drink of the wine of the wrath of God, which is poured out without mixture into the cup of his indignation; and he shall be tormented with fire and brimstone in the presence of the holy angels, and in the presence of the Lamb: And the smoke of their torment ascendeth up for ever and ever: and they have no rest day nor night, who worship the beast and his image, and whosoever receiveth the mark of his name". (Revelation 14:8-11)*

Further proof is documented in the book of Revelation. John went on to say, *"And there came one of the seven angels which had the seven vials, and talked with me, saying unto me, Come hither; I will show unto thee the judgment of the great whore that sitteth upon many waters: with whom the kings of the earth have committed fornication, and the inhabitants of the earth have been made drunk with the wine of her fornication.*

*So he carried me away in the spirit into the wilderness: and I saw a woman sit upon a scarlet coloured beast, full of blasphemy, having seven heads and ten horns. And the woman was arrayed in purple and scarlet colour, and decked with gold and precious stones and pearls, having a golden cup in her hand full of abominations and filthiness of her fornication.*

*And upon her forehead was a name written, MYSTERY, BABYLON THE GREAT, THE MOTHER OF HARLOTS AND ABOMINATIONS OF THE EARTH.*

*And I saw the woman drunken with the blood of the saints, and the martyrs of Jesus: and when I saw her, I wondered with great admiration. And the angel said unto me, Wherefore didst thou marvel? I will tell thee the mystery of the woman, and of the beast that carrieth her, which hath the seven heads and ten horns.*

*The beast that thou sawest was, and is not; and shall ascend out of the bottomless pit, and go into perdition: and they that dwell on the earth shall wonder, whose names were not written in the book of life from the foundation of the world, when they behold the beast that was, and is not, and yet is.*

*And here is the mind which hath wisdom. The seven heads are seven mountains, on which the woman sitteth. And there are seven kings': five are fallen, and one is, and the other is not yet come; and when he cometh, he must continue a short space.*

*And the beast that was and is not, even he is the eighth, and is of the seven, and goeth into perdition. And the ten horns which thou sawest are ten kings, which have received no kingdom as yet; but receive power as kings one hour with the beast. These have one mind, and shall give their power and strength unto the beast.*

*These shall make war with the Lamb, and the Lamb shall overcome them: for he is Lord of lords, and King of kings: and they that are with him are called, and chosen, and faithful.*

*And he saith unto me, the waters which thou sawest, where the whore sitteth, are peoples, and multitudes, and nations, and tongues.*

*And the ten horns which thou sawest upon the beast, these shall hate the whore, and shall make her desolate and naked, and shall eat her flesh, and burn her with fire. For God hath put in their hearts to fulfil his will, and to agree, and give their kingdom unto the beast, until the words of God shall be fulfilled.*

*And the woman which thou sawest is that great city, which reigneth over the kings of the earth." (Revelation 17:1-18)*

Rome, the seat of Paganism, the mother of the Catholic Church is thus depicted in Bible prophecy. It is well known that Rome is built upon seven mountains. **"The speech of the Romans is from the first Latin. The oldest gods of Rome - Saturn, Janus, Jupiter, Juno, Diana, & c. - are all Latin" (Encyclopaedia Britannica, Ninth Edition, Vol. 20, page 731).** These were all Pagan gods which were worshipped long before Constantine came to power and were the reigning deity of Rome in 325 AD.

The months of the Roman calendar took their names from these Pagan gods until this day. False Christianity continues to use these Pagan gods names instead of those of Judaic/Christian origin. God declared it an abomination to even mention the names of Pagan gods, yet false Christianity teaches us to acknowledge these Pagan gods by voicing their names daily.

The Catholic Church is the offspring of Rome, The Mother of Harlots. The Catholic Church calls itself the "Mother Church" of

Christianity. The reason behind this is that the Catholic Church has spawned most all of the church groups that call themselves Christian. Almost all of them are either directly or indirectly offshoots of the Catholic Church. Just like human families, you can recognize the inherited characteristics. All churches that follow certain traditions, customs and doctrines can easily be identified as having attributes received from the mother church.

Some of these attributes are as follows:

1. Doctrine of the "Trinity" (Polytheism)
2. Water Baptism by sprinkling
3. The Eucharist of Holy Communion
4. The cross as a Christian symbol (Pagan custom)
5. The fish as a Christian symbol (Pagan custom)
6. Eternal burning Hell (Dante's Inferno)
7. The celebration of Christmas (Pagan Feast of Sol)
    (a.) The Christmas tree
    (b.) The Yule log
    (c.) The wassail bowl
    (d.) Santa Claus
    (e.) Christmas candles
8. The celebration of Easter (Holy day for Sex Goddess)
    (a.) Easter eggs
    (b.) Easter Rabbits
    (c.) Easter sunrise service
9. The church steeple (Pagan Phallic symbol)
10. Ecclesiastical hierarchy of church government.
11. The celebration of Mardi Gras
12. The celebration of Lent.
13. The celebration of Halloween (satanic worship)
14. The veneration of statues or images.

15. Infant Baptism

16. Celibacy

The above attributes as religious practices all stem from Paganism or were originated by Catholicism; and not based on the Holy Scriptures. They are all practiced as traditions of the Catholic Church. Absolutely none of them were advocated by Christ or his Apostles for the followers of Christ.

Those churches that practice any of these attributes are not true followers of Christ and his Apostles; but are unwitting followers of the syncretism of Constantine's false Christianity.

Apostle Paul said, *"Be ye not unequally yoked together with unbelievers: for what fellowship hath righteousness with unrighteousness? and what concord hath Christ with Belial? or what part hath he that believeth with an infidel? And what agreement hath the temple of God with idols? For ye are the temple of the living God; as God hath said, I will dwell in them, and walk in them; and I will be their God, and they shall be my people.*

*Wherefore come out from among them, and be ye separate, saith the Lord, and touch not the unclean thing; and I will receive you, and will be a Father unto you, and ye shall be my sons and daughters, saith the Lord Almighty." (II Corinthians 6:14-18)*

The time has come to reveal the truth about the greatest hoax ever perpetrated against mankind. The end of Constantine's false Christianity is fast coming to pass. The mother church and her offspring will no longer represent Christ. True Christianity will flourish and overcome the sheep in wolves clothing.

John continues his prophecy, saying, *"And after these things I saw another angel come down from heaven, having great power; and the earth was lightened with his glory. And he cried mightily with a strong voice, saying, Babylon the great is fallen, is fallen, and is become the habitation of devils, and the hold of every foul spirit, and a cage of every unclean and hateful bird.*

*For all nations have drunk of the wine of the wrath of her fornication, and the kings of the earth have committed fornication with her, and the merchants of the earth are waxed rich through the abundance of her delicacies. And I heard another voice from heaven, saying, Come out of her, my people, that ye be not partakers of her sins, and that ye receive not of her plagues.*

*For her sins have reached unto heaven, and God hath remembered her iniquities. Reward her even as she rewarded you, and double unto her double according to her works: in the cup which she hath filled fill to her double.*

*How much she hath glorified herself, and lived deliciously, so much torment and sorrow give her: for she saith in her heart, I sit a queen, and am no widow, and shall see no sorrow. Therefore shall her plagues come in one day, death, and mourning, and famine; and she shall be utterly burned with fire: for strong is the Lord God who judgeth her.*

*And the kings of the earth, who have committed fornication and lived deliciously with her, shall bewail her, and lament for her, when they shall see the smoke of her burning, Standing afar off for the fear of her torment, saying, Alas, alas, the great city Babylon, that mighty city! for in one hour is thy judgment come.*

*And the merchants of the earth shall weep and morn over her; for no man buyeth their merchandise any more: The merchandise of gold, and silver, and precious stones, and of pearls, and fine linen, and purple, and silk, and scarlet, and all thyne wood, and all manner vessels of ivory, and all manner vessels of most precious wood, and of brass, and iron, and marble, And cinnamon, and odours, and ointments, and frankincense, and wine, and oil, and fine flour, and wheat, and beasts, and sheep, and horses, and chariots, and slaves, and souls of men.*

*And the fruits that thy soul lusted after are departed from thee, and all things which were dainty and goodly are departed from thee, and thou shalt find them no more at all. The merchants of these things, which were made rich by her, shall stand afar off for the fear of her torment, weeping and wailing, And saying, Alas, alas, that great city, that was clothed in fine linen, and purple, and scarlet, and decked with gold, and precious stones, and pearls!*

*For in one hour so great riches is come to nought. And every shipmaster, and all the company in ships, and sailors, and as many as trade by sea, stood afar off, And cried when they saw the smoke of her burning, saying, What city is like unto this great city!*

*And they cast dust on their heads, and cried, weeping and wailing, saying, Alas, alas, that great city, wherein were made rich all that had ships in the sea by reason of her costliness! for in one hour is she made desolate. Rejoice over her, thou heaven, and ye holy apostles and prophets; for God hath avenged you on her.*

*And a mighty angel took up a stone like a great millstone, and cast it into the sea, saying, Thus with violence shall that great city Babylon be thrown down, and shall be found no more at all. And the voice of harpers, and musicians, and of pipers, and trumpeters, shall be heard no more at all in thee; and no craftsman, of whatsoever craft he be, shall be found any more in thee; and the sound of a millstone shall be heard no more at all in thee; And the light of a candle shall shine no more at all in thee; and the voice of the bridegroom and of the bride shall be heard no more at all in thee: for thy merchants were the great men of the earth; for by thy sorceries were all nations deceived. And in her was found the blood of prophets, and of saints, and of all that were slain upon the earth.*

*And after these things I heard a great voice of much people in heaven, saying, Alleluia; Salvation, and glory, and honour, and power, unto the Lord our God: For true and righteous are his judgments: for he hath judged the great whore, which did corrupt the earth with her fornication, and hath avenged the blood of his servants at her hand.*

*And again they said, Alleluia. And her smoke rose up for ever and ever. And the four and twenty elders and the four beasts fell down and worshipped God that sat on the throne, saying, Amen; Alleluia.*

*And a voice came out of the throne, saying, Praise our God, all ye his servants, and ye that fear him, both small and great. And I heard as it were the voice of a great multitude, and as the voice of many waters, and as the voice of mighty thunderings, saying, Alleluia: for the Lord God omnipotent reigneth.*

*Let us be glad and rejoice, and give honour to him: for the marriage of the Lamb is come, and his wife hath made herself ready. And to her was granted that she should be arrayed in fine linen, clean and white: for the fine linen is the righteousness of saints.*

*And he saith unto me, Write, Blessed are they which are called unto the marriage supper of the Lamb. And he saith unto me, These are the true sayings of God. And I fell at his feet to worship him. And he said unto me, See thou do it not: I am thy fellowservant, and of thy brethren that have the testimony of Jesus: worship God: for the testimony of Jesus is the spirit of prophecy.*

*And I saw heaven opened, and behold a white horse; and he that sat upon him was called Faithful and True, and in righteousness he doth judge and make war. His eyes were as a flame of fire, and on his head were many crowns; and he had a name written, that no man knew, but he himself.*

*And he was clothed with a vesture dipped in blood: and his name is called The Word of God. And the armies which were in heaven followed him upon white horses, clothed in fine linen, white and clean.*

*And out of his mouth goeth a sharp sword, that with it he should smite the nations: and he shall rule them with a rod of iron: and he treadeth the winepress of the fierceness and wrath of Almighty God. And he hath on his vesture and on his thigh a name written. KING OF KINGS, AND LORD OF LORDS.*

*And I saw an angel standing in the sun; and he cried with a loud voice, saying to all the fowls that fly in the midst of heaven, Come and gather yourselves together unto the supper of the great God; That ye may eat the flesh of kings, and the flesh of captains, and the flesh of mighty men, and the flesh of horses, and of them that sit on them, and the flesh of all men, both free and bond, both small and great.*

*And I saw the beast, and the kings of the earth, and their armies, gathered together to make war against him that sat on the horse, and against his army. And the beast was taken, and with him the false prophet that wrought miracles before him, with which he deceived them that had received the mark of the beast, and them that worshipped his image. These both were cast alive into a lake of fire burning with brimstone.*

*And the remnant were slain with the sword of him that sat upon the horse, which sword proceeded out of his mouth: and all the fowls were filled with their flesh." (Revelation 18:1-19:21)*

The wisdom of Solomon says it all, *"Let us hear the conclusion of the whole matter: Fear God, and keep his commandments: for this is the whole duty of man. For God shall bring every work into judgment, with every secret thing, whether it be good, or whether it be evil." (Ecclesiastes 12:13-14)*

The End